CW00336852

JAGUAR

A FOULIS Motoring Book

First published, by Frederick Warne, in 1984
Reprinted by G. T. Foulis & Co., 1986, 1987 & 1988
Second edition published 1990
Reprinted 1990 & 1991
Third edition published 1995
Reprinted 1997

G. T. Foulis & Co. is an imprint of
Haynes Publishing,
Sparkford, Near Yeovil, Somerset BA22 7JJ

Tel: 01963 440635   Fax: 01963 440001
Int. tel: +44 1963 440635   Fax: +44 1963 440001
E-mail: sales@haynes-manuals.co.uk
Web site: http:/www.haynes.com

Haynes North America, Inc.
861 Lawrence Drive, Newbury Park,
California 91320 USA

British Library Cataloguing in Publication Data
A catalogue record for this book is available from the British
Library

ISBN 0-85429-962-9

Library of Congress catalog card number 95-77382

Printed and bound in Great Britain by
Butler & Tanner Ltd, Frome and London

JAGUAR
The Complete Illustrated History

Philip Porter

Foulis

Haynes

CONTENTS

ACKNOWLEDGEMENTS

As this is my first book I have particularly appreciated the kind and generous help given to me by a number of people.

Firstly I should like to record my gratitude to my old friend Nick Baldwin whose idea it originally was and who helped throughout with advice, photographs and moral support. Jeff Groman of Warnes has shown much patience and assisted greatly.

Regarding photographs Bob Taylor, Bertie Bradnack, David Grounds, Jack Fairman, Mrs. J. B. Parker, Mrs. Bayne, Mrs. E. Nicholson, Mrs. E. Simms, Mr. R. Gore, Don Smith and Mrs. M. W. F. Longlands have all very kindly lent me examples from their private collections. John Owen, Walter Gibbs in his role as Midland Automobile Club Archivist, and Mrs. Gill Hughes latterly of P. J. Evans have all given valued assistance; and Hugh Conway, Gil Mond and Geoff Walker have all helped with photographs and information. With regard to copying of ancient prints, et cetera, Ian Kerr and Graham Willey have been most helpful. Terry Moore of Phoenix Engineering has been a mine of information, and Jeremy Wade and Keith Stewart have both given me the benefit of their advice.

Above all I sincerely thank Alan Hodge, Steve Gilhooly, Norman Dewis and Roger Clinkscales for the tremendous part that they have played in the production of this volum Alan has as ever been his helpful self, with advice, phot information and introductions. My old chum Gil has help enormously checking the text for blunders and bringing l encyclopaedic Jaguar knowledge to my advantage. Norm spent hours talking to me, indeed fascinating me wi recollections from the fifties and sixties and lending me large part of his collection of photographs. Without Rog this book could not have been produced. He h responsibility for Jaguar's own collection of photograph apart from being kept very busy as head of the Photograph Department. In spite of his ever heavy workload he h helped me enormously, dealing with my many, and I am su tedious requests with patience and alacrity. Above all I ha greatly appreciated the trust he has shown in lending n many irreplaceable glass negatives.

Finally, I am mindful of the honour accorded me by bo Sir William Lyons and Mr Nick Scheele penning a piece f my modest offering. To them and their many other colleagu at Jaguar, my sincere thanks.

Philip Port

FOREWORD

by
The late Sir William Lyons, RDI
Former President of Jaguar Cars Ltd

I was very pleased to be asked by Mr. Porter to write this Foreword for this new book. It has given me great pleasure to see the enthusiasm of the Jaguar Drivers' Club grow, and my colleagues at Jaguar Cars Limited today will always be as pleased as I am to know that our efforts have resulted in such a strong following for the product, both new and old.

I am sure all readers of this book will appreciate their cars all the more for this insight into Jaguars now no longer produced, but current models will now perhaps be even more enjoyed as the Jaguar pedigree progresses.

INTRODUCTION

is book is not intended to be the definitive volume on the ject of Jaguar, nor is it intended to be a mere coffee table tion. Rather it is meant to be a reasonably comprehensive tory of the famous company that began as Swallow, became and then achieved worldwide success, respect and fame as uar.

he dramatic development of the famous Jaguar company m its humble origins as a manufacturer of sidecars through the present position of automotive eminence worldwide is d chronologically by model. Personal recollections of Jaguar sonalities are quoted, adding a human – and sometimes norous – slant to the history.

have treated the competition story separately from the tory of the production models, believing that to combine h would be to cloud each with too much detail. Treated arately, one can clearly see the development of each, but one uld always remember the beneficial effects competitive ticipation undoubtedly had upon the development of the d cars. Indeed, every Jaguar has had sporting pretensions, ne more pronounced than others, and it was (and still is) ntial that they took on the opposition in the sporting arenas the world. That they did so, and with such success in the os, created a foundation on which they have built to this day.

At the conclusion of the book there is a brief chapter on styling influences. Styling is such an emotive and subjective issue that everyone will have their own views and my ideas may be seen by some to be controversial. However, their purpose is simply to initiate discussion.

A very special feature of the book is the over 350 illustrations, almost all period shots that have not been seen before. It is becoming extremely difficult to find Swallow, SS and Jaguar photographs previously unseen and in this area I have been very fortunate to have been assisted greatly by the Jaguar company and several private individuals.

When I was first asked to write this book, the prospects for Jaguar looked dismal. There was a succession of fuel crises, poor labour relations, slipping standards and seemingly little direction, all of them threatening the extinction of a company living off its past. Now, happily, things look a lot brighter, and Jaguar have regained their self-respect and restored their name to worldwide prominence.

As the advertising slogan had it: 'the legend grows'. And this book charts the background and foundation of that legend, a legend created by good design, aggressive business leadership, styling flair, value for money and competitive success – all creating the evocative name of 'Jaguar'.

1 THE SWALLOW

From humble beginnings in 1922 as manufacturers of sidecars Lyons and
his partner's newly formed business progressed to rebodying motor cars.
Commencing with the ubiquitous Austin 7 the treatment was meted out
to a series of cars, the most significant of which was the Standard.
Meanwhile, sidecar production continued apace, being a useful
bread-and-butter line.

1

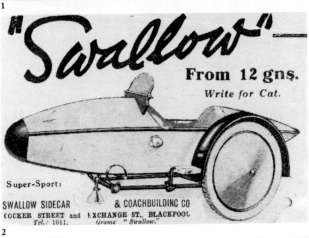

"Swallow"

From 12 gns.

Write for Cat.

Super-Sports

SWALLOW SIDECAR & COACHBUILDING CO
COCKER STREET and EXCHANGE ST., BLACKPOOL
Tel.: 1011.   Grams "Swallow."

2

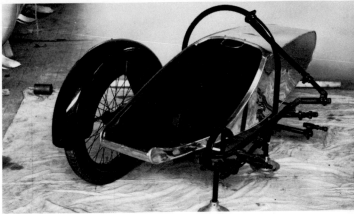

3

great story of Jaguar, and Sir Wil- [Ly]ons, begins with the name Swal- [low]. For in 1922, William Lyons (as he [the]n was) and William Walmsley formed [the] Swallow Sidecar Company, with [prem]ises in Bloomfield Street, Black- [poo]l. Young Lyons had been a [mot]orcycle enthusiast for a while and he [add]ed to this a certain eye for style and [a he]ad for business, both of which can [be] detected all the way through this [stor]y. It is likely that if this were a novel, [it w]ould be dismissed as a fairy tale, [bec]ause from these humble beginnings

Lyons built one of the greatest names the world of motoring has yet known, and is ever likely to know. In the field of growth, excellence, exports and international competitive events, Lyons's company was to achieve prominent success.

For the first 50 or so years this is the story of one man, a decisive, autocratic leader who by a combination of flair, acumen and downright hard work achieved so much. He was Sir William Lyons, who might be described as 'the man who has stolen more Motor Shows than any other'.

He started with just £1,000 and a few men and lads, and when he retired he left behind an empire, including such dis-

1 A Swallow Model 4 Super Sports sidecar, reminiscent of a Zeppelin (J C) 2 A 1928 Swallow sidecar advertisement (J C) 3 A racing 'chair' but still with Swallow's usual attention to style and finish (J C) 4 The Light Weight de Luxe, described by Swallow as the 'Sidecar for the Connoisseur' (J C) 5 This advertisement marked the beginning of the long relationship with Henlys, although their artist appears to have adopted considerable licence in the top illustration (J C)

The **SWALLOW** HAS ARRIVED!

SPORTS BODIES
for the Connoisseur

The perfection of body-building art developed upon new and better lines. Grace, exquisite finish, greater comfort and better protection, feature in all Swallow products.

HENLYS have been appointed Sole Distributors for the Southern Counties (excepting Kent), and are offering these striking bodies on specially tuned Austin 7 and Morris Chassis at the following attractive prices.

A fine selection of beautiful colour schemes is available. The features include cowl over radiator, Vee screen, draught-proof side curtains or coupe head, etc. For early delivery orders should be placed now.

These bodies transform the Austin into a real car—giving big car comfort and lines. The bodies on the Cowley Chassis introduce an entirely new Morris model.

The MORRIS Cowley Model

The AUSTIN 7 Swallow

PRICES:

	Swallow Austin	Swallow Morris
With cape hood only	£175	£220
With coupe saloon head only	£185	£230
With cape hood and interchangeable coupe saloon head	£190	£235

Send at once for Booklet giving full specifications or call and see these marvellous bodies at

HENLYS
SOLE SWALLOW DISTRIBUTORS FOR SOUTHERN ENGLAND (EXCEPT KENT)

| 1, 3 & 5, Peter St., Manchester Telephone: Central 1780 | 91, 155-157, GT. PORTLAND ST., W.1. Phone: Langham 1141 (10 lines). | DEVONSHIRE HOUSE, PICCADILLY. Phone: Grosvenor 2271 | Service Station : Hawley Cres ent, Camden Town. N.W.1 Hampstead 5177. |

5

tinguished names as Daimler, Coventry Climax, Guy and Meadows, but above all Jaguar, which became a household name. It is a name synonymous with speed, style and quality.

A man of whom the motoring press and his competitors continually asked, at the announcement of each new model, 'How does he do it at the price?', never really had to sell a car – his order books were virtually always full.

To his credit, he chose and employed some brilliant men whom he moulded into a great team. He understood the significance of competition success and realized the potential sales market across the Atlantic and proceeded to exploit it. Indeed, *The Motor* was moved to comment in its editorial leader of 16th November 1949, following the announcement of the XK120, its achievement of 132 mph at Jabbeke and its victory at

Silverstone, that: 'There is, surely, a lesson which transcends this immediate case of a high performance two-seater. It is that the export market will respond to a car having outstanding quality in its class and sold at a reasonable price. The average car is palpably more difficult to sell and it is evident that British designers must be guided by the motto "Aim Higher", and manufacturers must remember when competing with foreign makes the advice given by an admiral to a junior officer "My boy, if argument becomes heated about politics after dinner, and someone throws a glass of wine in your face, don't throw your wine in his: throw the decanter stopper." In the realm of highspeed motoring it is evident that Mr Lyons of Jaguar Cars has thrown a very heavy stopper very hard indeed.'

William Lyons was to throw many heavy stoppers in his long career. Just

before his 21st birthday, William Ly met William Walmsley, a man some r years his senior. Walmsley was p ducing, at the rate of one per week fr a brick outhouse behind his pare home, a rather striking sidecar which was fitting to war-surplus Triun motorcycles he had recondition Young Lyons detected a commer possibility with these sidecars wh brought style to what had previou been ugly attachments, if product could be raised to a more busines output.

Although they had to wait sev weeks for Lyons to come of a Walmsley and Lyons formed the Sw low Sidecar Co on 4th September 19 with a bank overdraft of £1,000 guar teed by their respective fathers. Initia they operated from the first and seco floors of an old building in Bloomfi

1

8

oad, Blackpool with several men and a oy, although their workforce quickly xpanded and further premises were quired.

The new company pioneered the use of luminium panelling and had their own and at the 1923 Motor Cycle Show. here they achieved the distinction ` having their 'chair' displayed on the ands of such august names as Brough uperior, Dot and Coventry Eagle.

A range of different models was fered, with a touring model costing 22 10s, and the most prestigious model ited, the Coupé de Luxe, at an extrava- nt £30. The orders flowed in, produc- on was raised, the workforce was creased to 30 and another move came necessary, this time to Cocker treet in 1926. These premises were rchased by Walmsley Snr and leased the company.

Demand and therefore production continued to grow, and about this time Lyons started to export – a field that was to assume greater and greater import- ance as the years rolled by. Meanwhile, in 1927, another exciting development attracted everyone's attention.

Herbert Austin, fighting the Depres- sion of the 1920s, had designed and introduced the legendary Austin Seven. As is well known, the car was intended to be cheap, economical and reliable to run, and easy to drive, thus bringing motoring to the masses. Lyons and Walmsley may have feared that this new concept might compete with their staple product, or maybe they just saw an opportunity for expansion. Whichever way it was, they grasped the initiative and launched a re-bodied version of the urbane Austin Seven.

There is a definite parallel between the

motorcars of the 1920s and those of recent years. As in the 1990s when mass-producers compete to make visu- ally duller and duller boxlike cars, so in the 1920s the majority of saloons were bodily austere and unadventurous. As in recent years specialist manufacturers who innovate and dare to be a little exciting achieve a vogue, big companies

1 *This 1929 model Austin Swallow Saloon shows the standard two-tone design, and it's easy to see why the bonnet colour scheme was referred to as the pen-nib.* 2 *A 1929 model of an Austin Swallow Two-Seater with the cape hood* (J C) 3 *A rear view shows the neatly rounded tail so characteristic of these models – note the open vent* (J C) 4 *Apart from the Austin Two-Seater, this factory advertisement illustrates the shortlived Morris Swallow Sports* (J C)

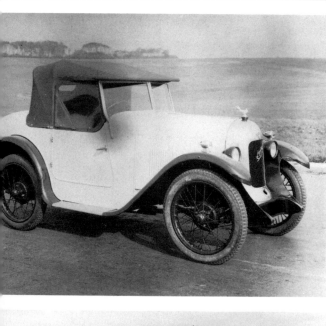

4

desperately market multitudinous options to attempt to disguise the uniformity of their products, and owners cherish quite bad cars from the past merely because they are different, so in the twenties there was a demand from people who wished to be a little individual; from those who wanted a car with some visual personality and modest elegance.

The Swallow range of cars was created to satisfy this demand. Lyons had again tried to bring style to the commonplace. The car had a delightful body constructed of heavy gauge aluminium over an ash frame and a wooden floor. A few early models had bicycle-type front wings that turned with the steering, and no running boards. But fuller wings and running boards were soon added, as you can see from the illustrations. The vulnerable wasp-shaped or beetle-shaped tail was aluminium but with no internal framework. The rear number plate was carried on brackets below, to which on the nearside, the two-inch copper-extended exhaust pipe was affixed. Some tails had professionally built hatches or lids for easy access, but this was not standard. A bullnose radiator graced the front. This item was originally aluminium, then nickel-plated steel and was finally chrome plated. The radiator shell carried the usual wings motif and a honeycomb grille on which was mounted centrally 'Austin Swallow' in script. An aluminium four-piece bonnet, centrally hinged, had 14 fluted vertical louvres on each side for engine ventilation.

The Austin Seven chassis was modified only by the addition on both sides of an angle iron, approximately the length of the running boards, upon which the main body timbers were bolted. A contemporary magazine noted that 'the brakes were as good as might be expected on so small a car, and when used in conjunction (hand and foot) could be termed efficient'!

A neat detachable hard-top (surely one of the earliest examples of this item, if not the earliest) known as the Coupé Saloon Head, could be hinged for easier access – a boon, surely, because the inside width of the body was a mere 38 inches. But after a while this was found to be impractical and the hard-top was merely bolted on.

In spite of these apparently constricting dimensions, Swallow felt able to state in one of their advertisements, 'It combines in ideal form the sweeping lines and performance of the sports car with the luxurious, roomy comfort of the big car – no wonder it is such a popular

success'. This was a good example of the company's advertising prose, showing absolutely no regard for modesty, and which was to be a continuing and fascinating theme in all factory brochures and advertisements. While the prewar period was renowned for its flowery promotional prose it seems that the company was pre-eminent even in this sphere.

Announced in 1927 some three months after the Austin, and produced into 1928, was the Swallow-bodied version of the Morris Cowley chassis with 1550 cc engine, known as the Morris Swallow Two-seater. Comparatively little is known about this particular model and it is thought that only a few were made. One theory to account for this was its resemblance to the current MG, which it bettered in price but could not compare with in performance. With Ace discs disguising the artillery wheels the price was £210, or £220 with wire wheels.

Externally, apart from being larger than the Austin, the body was less curvaceous, with a high bonnet line, V-shaped windscreen, side-mounted spare wheel and sloping tail incorporating a dickey seat.

To meet its changing role, the com

1

2

ny title was expanded in 1927 to read 'he Swallow Sidecar and Coachbuild-g Co.' About that time the first over-as agent, one Emil Frey of Zurich, was pointed, initially for the sale of side-rs, the production of which continued expand. In 1982 Emil Frey, at the age 83, had bestowed on him an honorary BE for his services to British exports.

In November 1928 the open two-ater version of the trusty Seven was pplemented by the addition of a saloon sed on the same chassis.

The company's catalogue stated that, he Sports Saloon, embodying the finement and exclusive distinction characteristic to the luxury car, makes a strong appeal to those of discriminating taste to whom such qualities are essen-tial. Grace of outline, perfect propor-tions, and exquisite colours, enhanced by seating accommodation for two adults and two or three juvenile passengers'.

The body, again aluminium over ash, had two doors with vertically sliding windows balanced by an internal spring-loaded roller. The window could be held in any position by a central locking lever. The roof was of wooden framework con-structed so that in later models a sun-shine roof could be fitted to order. Otherwise the top was covered with a black leatherette material. In the roof behind the rear passenger was a square four-inch air vent. The earlier saloons had solid wooden rear floorboards that produced in the passengers a 'knees

Foleshill in 1929, showing the creation of the Austin Swallows: **1** *Austin Saloon beginning to take shape with the construction of its wooden frame.* **2** *Part of the body shop.* **3** *Body frames, now panelled, ready for the paint-shop.* **4** *In the trim shop.* **5** *Now painted, exterior fittings begin to be added.* **6** *Nearing completion, to the left is the distinctive wasp-shaped tail of the Two-seater.* **7** *Completed, the little Swallows await delivery (J C)*

6

7

under their chins' attitude. Later, a metal well was fitted with a central hump to house the propellor shaft. The roof forepeak was curved forward, projecting by four inches in front of the windscreen centre V point and 1½ inches at the side posts.

The 'exquisite' colour schemes were, to say the least, bold for the depressed 1920s. The catalogue listed the following 'exceptionally highly polished: Cream and Crimson; Grey and Green; Light Mole Brown and Deep Suede Brown; Ivory and Black; Cherry Red and Maroon; Sky Blue and Danish Blue; Cream and Violet; Birch Grey and Battleship Grey; Ivory and Dark Blue. The first mentioned colour in each case alludes to the body below the waistline; the latter to the wings, wheels, chassis and head above the waistline'.

And if that did not convince the ladies who were attracted to the Swallow Seven, then this further extract from the sales catalogue probably did: 'THE INTERIOR FURNISHINGS are artistically finished in polished mahogany or walnut, the instrument fascia board being neatly mounted with switchbox, ammeter, speedometer, and oil pressure gauge. Incorporated in the design is an artistically designed locker, providing Ladies Companion Set. The floor coverings are of pile carpet, in colours [to] match the upholstery. An interior electric light with tumbler switch is fitted into the roof, and an adjustable mirror provides clear vision through the rear window light.'

As to sales, Parkers had been appointed distributors for Manchester, and Brown and Mallalieu for Blackpool, when Lyons decided to take one of his new Austin Swallows down to visit the comparatively new firm of Henlys in London. To his surprise and delight Henlys said that they would take 50 provided they could be the sole distributors

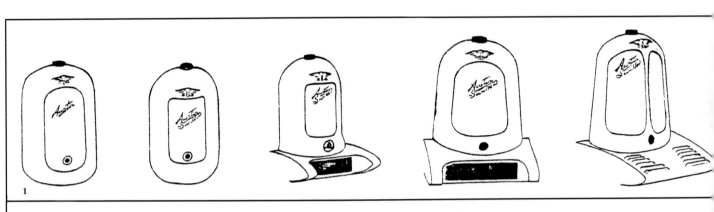

1

2

12

utors for the south of England. To s Lyons agreed and set off back ndering how on earth he was going to ld the high number of 500 cars. For this reason, and because the side- production was still expanding, other move became necessary. A sup- f of suitably skilled workers was the rriding factor, so Coventry, being the rt of the motor industry, was chosen, i there they would have the added vantage of being nearer to their sup- ers. An old munitions factory at Hol- ok Lane, Foleshill, was found to be table and the move was made. It was rave move in 1928, when many com-

panies were going to the wall. Ironically, the Depression probably helped Swallow rather than hindered it, for those who had been used to expensive individually coachbuilt cars found the Swallow within even their impoverished means and, more to the point, it seemed less of a come-down.

In 1930 the Mark II version of the Swallow Seven appeared at the Motor Show with minor revisions. The radiator shell was less bull-nosed and more V-shaped, and had a vertical chrome strip down the centre. The bonnet, an inch-and-a-half longer, now boasted 30 louvres on each side, and most Mark II

models had front and rear bumpers. Upholstery was of real leather, interior trimmings were plated throughout and the furnishings were of polished mahogany. Further additions included adjust-

1 Evolution of the Austin Swallow radiator, 1927–1932 (Swallow Register) 2 The Swallow treatment worked equally happily on the larger Fiat chassis (J C) 3 A fine example of Henlys' audacious advertising style, featuring a Standard 9 after Swallow treatment. 4 A badge evolved for the Standard, with perhaps a hint of what was to come. 5 Another illustration of Henlys' 'modesty' when applied to other Swallow products (J C)

able front bucket seats, a rear blind with driver's control, Bakelite ignition and throttle-control levers, and a Yale-type door lock incorporated in the door handles.

In a period advertisement Swallow felt able to state that the revised car made 'an irresistible appeal to discriminating motorists', and the new features contributed to 'harmonizing to create one of the most outstanding small cars of the generation'.

This model continued to be very popular and the false dumb irons were copied by other manufacturers. In January 1930, HH The Sultan of Perak took delivery of a Swallow Seven Saloon, appropriately finished in purple and black.

Visitors to the Motor Show of 1929 would have noted on the Swallow stand not only the familiar Austin but also no fewer than three new models. These were based on the Fiat Tipo 509A, the Standard Big Nine and the Swift Ten.

Walmsley had at first a Clyno and later an Alvis, bodied by the company for his own use. The company was always on the lookout for a new chassis for the Swallow treatment, especially after Lyons had been snubbed by Sir Herbert Austin. James Ritchie, later a Jaguar distributor, supplied the Fiat chassis, for which he was the Glasgow agent. Ritchie therefore approached Lyons suggesting that the Fiat might be suitable for the Swallow treatment.

The Fiat, like the others, was simply an enlarged version of the Austin Swallow theme. From the rear the two cars were very similar, but frontal treatment differed from model to model. The Fiat 9 hp chassis with an engine of 990 cc made a pleasant sporting saloon of modest performance. It had two doors and four seats, the rear ones being sunk below the chassis to give extra leg room. Production of this model ceased during 1930 after, it is thought, between 50 and 70 had been completed.

Most significant of the trio first seen at the 1929 Motor Show was the 9 hp Standard Swallow, for not only did it stay in production rather longer than the other two, with a consequently greater number being produced, but it began an association with the Standard Motor Company that was to assume greater and greater importance.

'The grace of line', claimed the brochure, 'appeals to the artistic taste.' Furthermore, the sales patter continued, 'The interior appointments signify the dignified refinements characteristic of the luxury car. The spacious lounge seats, heavily carpeted floors and polished mahogany furnishings enhance the superlative exterior finish.'

The most notable external difference from the other models was a new chromium-plated radiator shell slightly raked to the rear with a central bar coming down to meet the louvred tray between the dumb irons. The driver's windscreen 'opened if required when driving in fog or for ventilation', and a suction-operated screen-wiper was fitted to the lower part.

Considering its high standard of finish and range of appointments the Big Nine was not expensive at £245. 'In fact', claimed the company, 'there is no car, regardless of price, so fascinatingly attractive.' The following optional extras could be specified: Splintex glass for £10, a rear blind for 10/6d or front and rear double bumpers at five guineas.

A reader of one of the motori[ng] journals wrote to the magazine in 19[xx] that she was the proud possessor of [the] first Standard Swallow to be put on [the] road. 'I gave my car a very care[ful] running-in for well over 1,000 mil[es] then I set off complete with husba[nd] friend, dog, portable wireless, th[ree] large and heavy suit-cases, also [a] superabundance of fishing tackle, to s[ay] nothing of three pairs of rubber bo[ots] (very bulky articles these) and a f[ew] other little odds and ends, for some ri[ver] and lake fishing in mountainous Wal[es]. The car behaved (as every lady shou[ld] perfectly, and revelled in showing t[he] world that long and winding "one-i[n]-sixes" were the joy of its life, also th[at] it could jog along at a steady 45 mph [all] day and all night.

'Speed on top is about 57 mph b[ut]

1

2

en good conditions, a mile or so more ...y be added. On second it is possible ... attain 32 to 35 mph, but it is not ...ommended. While on the subject of ...rs, I should mention that to anyone ... used to the Standard gear-change a ...le practice is necessary before it can ...made quite silently.

I find acceleration good, and in ...ond gear very good. Petrol consump-...n works out at about 35 mpg at ...mph. Easy starting. Good brakes. I ...e no grumble worth mentioning, and ...d my Standard Swallow a very reli-...e little car.'

...The Swift Swallow was based on the ...ift 'Fleetwing' chassis fitted with a ...0 cc engine. It had the usual Swallow ...inements and many of the improve-...nts introduced in the Swallow Austin ...1930, namely – leather upholstery,

polished mahogany and double panel V windscreen. Two large doors gave good access to front and rear seats, the occupants of the latter benefiting from deep footwells. The usual adventurous colours were available plus Swallow Apple Green and Swallow Deep Leaf Green. Green, it was said, was a most hard-wearing colour, and it is interesting to note that the company paint shop mounted the drums of paint on electric motors, thereby agitating the liquid and maintaining consistency of shade.

The demise of the Swift concern in 1931 caused the cessation of this model after something like 150 had been produced at a price of £283 8s od each.

The relationship with Standard took a further step forward in May 1931 with the introduction of a Swallow-bodied 16 hp six-cylinder Enfield, which was

priced at £275, with the optional sliding roof. In almost every way the car was identical to its smaller-engined brother. It is believed that 56 of these 'Ensign' Swallows were built, but the significance of the model was that it led to the company's acquaintance with the smooth, reliable 2054 cc sidevalve engine with its

1 *From March 1930 Swallow built a limited number of saloons based on the Swift Ten (J C)* 2 *The larger Standard served to introduce Swallow to the trusty Six, referred to in advertisements as a 15 hp* 3 *The most prominent feature of the Two-Seater Hornet was this pretty tail-end treatment, bravely flamboyant for the austere 1930s – seen here taking part in a Bugatti Club treasure hunt*

impressive 7-bearing crankshaft. To Lyons and Walmsley this sturdy engine seemed ideal for a project they had in mind.

Production at that stage was running at a good 100 cars per week, with the Austin Saloon still going strong. Indeed, the price was reduced from £187 10s 0d to just £165 for the saloon, and £150 for the two-seater with Coupé hood only, or £160 with the Coupé Saloon head only. Also, the list of optional extras was growing.

An ingenious little production line had been set up at the Coventry factory. The timber from the drying room passed through a special French machine which planed it on both sides, and thence into a circular saw. All wooden pieces were made with such precision that no alterations were necessary when they came to be assembled on jigs. As a result, eight lads could assemble more than 30 saloon frames a day. The panelling process took rather longer because of the need to eliminate every blemish that might be shown up by the high gloss cellulose which by then was standard.

A good chassis with lively performance successfully married to an exceptionally good-looking body, even by Lyons's standards, sums up the Swallow Hornet two-seater, launched in 1930. A number of contributors to the correspondence columns of the motoring press suggested that it was 'the most attractive small car on the road'.

The hood, quite shapely when erected, was completely concealed when folded, although it needed some practice to do this quickly and neatly. Two spare wheels, rather generous for a small car modestly priced at £225, were standard and they were mounted on strong brackets on either side of the bonnet. The seat back rest which was not adjustable (to the chagrin of shorter drivers), hinged forward to reveal quite a large locker in the tail. The model sold well and continued in production until 1932.

A four-seater version of the Hornet

1

2

Announcing the 1933
SWALLOW HORNET
●

1932 has given ample evidence of the popularity of Swallow Hornets. Now we are proud to introduce their 1933 successors—even more beautiful—with added refinements—and definite improvements.

Pictured below is the sparkling two-seater priced at . . . £255

SWALLOW COACHBUILDING CO. LTD.
FOLESHILL, COVENTRY (Coventry 8027)

SWALLOW HORNET

3

s listed from 1931. The rear end treat-
nt was more traditional, with one
r-mounted spare wheel. The single
ne windscreen was well raked and had
angular side panels. With comfort in
nd, the newly designed front seats had
shions with a nine-inch front, which
re good support beneath the knees.
e hood folded neatly and lay horizon-
ly. Wings were close-fitting and had
igh domed section for both style and
ength.

In 1930 one of the magazines noted
he Swallow Morris Minor – an experi-
nt recently seen at Henly's Ltd,
ston Road', although this was purely
ne-off.

In 1932 Wolsley announced the extensively modified 'Hornet Special', and
Swallow continued with the two- and
four-seater bodies to clothe this new
variation.

The Wolsley company's philosophy
was stated as follows: 'It is implied that
the chassis is not sold as a racing job, but
as a basis which is structurally correct
and upon which keen coachbuilders can
develop whatever they desire for the
capability of high performance is present
in the design; and all the much desired
refinements for speed work are already
incorporated.'

The bodies were identical to the
previous models, 'the long lines (of the

two-seater) emphasized by the narrow
beading with the double lozenge beneath
the windscreen'. A bare chassis would
have cost you £180 and with Swallow
two-seater coachwork a further £75, the
four-seater being just £5 dearer.

*1 The Four-Seater clearly lost the style of the
Two-Seater, with its average tail treatment 2
The Swallow Hornets continued to be produced
concurrently with the early SSs (J C) 3 The
frontal treatment meted out by Lyons to the
Hornet Two-Seater – the Special was
announced in 1932*

2 THE SS MARQUE

Just nine years from its inception the company evolved from mere 're-bodiers' to motor manufacturers. The SS marque achieved considerable publicity and created an affordable style that carried the company through the difficult thirties; and a stronger and most important symbiotic trading relationship was created with the Standard Motor Company.

William Lyons's ambition was to build his own cars rather than merely re-body other people's, for the latter necessarily places certain constraints upon your designs. To have a completely free hand you must produce your own chassis, and this he did in 1931 with the introduction of the SS I Coupé. The car caused quite a stir at its introduction at the 1931 Motor Show, because it had the look of a car costing £1,000 or more, yet it was listed at a mere £310. Lyons had once more brought style within easy reach of the motoring masses. A smaller model – the SS II – was also offered. The chassis and engine for both these cars were supplied by the Standard Motor Company, and it was said to be the first time that a chassis had been designed by a body-builder.

The initials SS have variously been ascribed to Standard Swallow, Standard Special, Swallow Sports, and Swallow Sidecars, but it was never really decided what it did stand for – it depended whether you worked for Standard or Swallow. The title may well have been borrowed from the famous Brough Superior SS 80 and SS 90 motor cycles.

A variety of body styles was very popular but, sadly, the performance of the car never really lived up to the expectations created by the sporty appearance.

1 *Formed in the early 1930s, the SS Car Club flourished until the outbreak of the war. This montage shows a good cross-section of models* (J C) 2–6 *'WAIT!', the advertisements had proclaimed in mid-1931, 'The SS is coming,' and on 9th October it duly arrived* (Mrs M. W. F. Longlands)7 *A number of non-original additions (headlamps, horns, etc) make this a rather strange example of the very rare SS II Coupé, but it serves to show the overall shape* (National Motor Museum)

6

The car was unkindly parodied with slogans such as Soda Squirt and Super Sexed, but those ungracious people were going to have to eat their words in a few years' time.

'The SS is coming', announced the company's advertisement in the autumn of 1931. The new range, announced on 9th October, first appeared at the Olympia Motor Show later the same month. 'Long, low and rakishly sporting' was the press reaction. 'Boldly individualistic – daring to be different' claimed the SS catalogue.

By mounting the engine several inches farther back in the chassis than in the comparable Standard, and by lengthening the wheelbase and mounting the springs alongside the frame rather than under it, was the way in which Lyons was able to design such a low body for the period. This, plus the length of the bonnet, which was at least half as long as the whole car, contributed to its sporty appearance or producing, as one writer bluntly described it, 'a real cad's car'.

The frame was an entirely new design of the double-dropped type. From parallel dumb irons, the side members splayed out about two-thirds along the engine, whence they continued along parallel lines again. Level with the gearbox, the frame swept down $2\frac{1}{2}$ inches and

then up again over the back axle. The side members were adequately cro braced at various points. As alrea mentioned, the road springs were mou ted alongside the chassis, and at the re they were slung under the axle casin This was a Standard component equi ped with special hubs to allow the fitti of Rudge-Whitworth 'racing-type' w wheels, shod with $5\frac{1}{2} \times 18$-in Dunl tyres. The steering box, again Standard manufacture, was fitted w forward to enable the column to almost horizontal, resulting in the des able near vertical steering wheel.

All these modifications to the norn Standard chassis were designed in t

rests of the ultra-low body. The result was successful. A man of average height could, while standing, comfortably rest his elbow on the roof, yet have adequate headroom when driving.

What the 16 hp Standard lacked in d performance it made up for in rdiness, smoothness and torque. ep gradients presented no problem, the SS would accelerate without fuss n 5 mph in top. The low body iously meant a low centre of gravity, ch contributed to the above average dholding. This was aided by the t, responsive steering and commented by the easy SS-designed gear nge mounted on the Standard 4-

speed box. Both hand and foot brakes operated on all four wheels. Soon after its introduction, the SS I could also be had with the Standard 20 hp side-valve engine of 2552 cc.

The imposing radiator was V-shaped, slightly raked and surrounded by two large Lucas headlamps that were carried on a curved tie rod connecting the domed wings. The deep sides of the extravagantly long bonnet were covered with a plethora of louvres. Two large doors gave good access to the interior, which consisted of a wide bench just capable of carrying three adults, and a cramped rear seat adequate for luggage, two children or one adult at a pinch.

The rather heavy rear quarters of the roof were relieved by dummy 'pram

1 The advent of the SS I once again gave the advertising copywriters full reign to exercise their verbosity (J C) 2 The SS I Saloon must have been considerably less claustrophobic for the rear seat passengers (J C) 3 An unusual rear view of the SS I Coupé showing the generously proportioned luggage locker 4 An SS I Coupé with one or two interesting extras, including the tinted sunshade (Mrs M. W. F. Longlands) 5 The SS I Tourer allowed the whole family to enjoy open-air motoring (N. Baldwin) 6 Proof that the SS I Tourer was indeed a full four-seater, with presumably a good deal of comfort (J C) 7 The SS I Coupé in its 1933 guise; with its flowing wing line it was a more balanced design

6

irons', and to the rear was mounted a luggage locker and the spare wheel. A flush-fitting sliding roof was provided, and this and the rest of the roof were covered in black fabric. The car could be ordered in primrose with black wings and chassis or, if you preferred, lake and carnation red.

The SS II was simply a smaller version of the larger SS I and, as such, was inevitably overshadowed. That was rather a shame because, although it was a modest little car, it has come to be more highly respected with hindsight. Writing in the early 1970s a motoring scribe was moved to comment, 'The little SS is surprisingly nice to drive, bearing in mind that comfort is subordinate to styling ... top speed is 60 mph if you're patient'. Based on a modified version of the Standard Little Nine chassis with a 9 hp engine of 1006 cc, it was priced at £210. It was purely a two-seater and although it lacked performance – 10 to 40 mph in top took 25 seconds – its fuel economy somewhat compensated for this with a consumption of 38 mpg and oil quoted at 2000 mpg.

The financial depression of the 1930s seemed to have little or no effect on SS sales, because the SS was probably the lowest-priced car available that gave the appearance of being expensively coachbuilt. And it was looks that still impressed many people in the 1930s.

To put into context the new SSs against their opposition, a 1932 price guide showed that the SS II at £210 was £5 dearer than the Standard Nine, £10 less than the Trojan and the comparable Renault, £18 less than the Rover Ten Special and £25 cheaper than the Hillman Aero Minx. The SS I 16 hp at £325, and the 20 hp at £335 compared with the Lanchester at £315, the six-cylinder Essex and four-cylinder Rhode at £315 apiece, the 16 hp Wolseley and the 19.9 hp Standard at the same price, the Chrysler Plymouth and Star at £345, and the Hillman Wizard, Morris Isis and Rover Speed Pilot all at £350.

For 1933 the SS I was revised to keep pace with fashion and improve on the previous model's shortcomings. The wheelbase and track were increased by 7 inches and 2 inches respectively, and the extra length was utilized in the rear seat area, allowing the previously cramped accommodation to be occupied by two adults, and therefore widening the market for this model. To enable this use of the back seats, the chassis was also modified, being underslung at the rear, passing under the axle and having triangulated cross braces. The rear seating area was treated in a novel way,

because the propshaft split the back seats due to the low level of the body in relation to the axle, so the rear seat was sculptured like two armchairs. It is said, though unlikely to be true, that their design was based on the office chairs at Foleshill.

The individual helmet-type wings of the earlier model gave way to the continuous flowing type with running boards incorporated. And the tie-bar to which the headlamps had been attached

was deleted, the lamps now being affi directly onto the wings. Performa was increased a little by fitt aluminium heads to the trusty 16 hp 20 hp engines, giving a higher comp sion ratio. Either a Solex or RAG-t carburettor and engine-driven pump supplied petrol from the enlar 12-gallon tank. A new design of radi block and enlarged bonnet louvres v increased protrusion aided cooling.

On the road the SS I's strong p

s still its cornering, particularly at
her speeds. The long, flat, semi-
ptic springs gave a firm, yet not harsh,
e. A curved top panel to the opening
gle-pane windscreen improved
ion, and the rear passengers, who had
le or no vision, if suffering from
ustrophobia could now at least have
ne ventilation from the opening rear
dow. Some relief could also be
ned from new scuttle-mounted venti-
ors, while extensive use of felt around

the bulkhead was intended to keep
engine fumes out.

The upholstery, as before, was
covered in Vaumol hide, and the front
seats, now bucket-type, could be easily
adjusted on their ball bearing slides. The
tools that were formerly carried beneath
the dash were now moved to the lid of
the luggage trunk. Generally, the SS I
had matured into a more balanced and
practical car, yet with its distinctive
individuality unmarred.

Another model was introduced in the
spring of 1933, namely the SS I Tourer.
This open four-seater had a pleasing
appearance when in open guise, but the
line suffered when the hood was raised.
However, it gave a hint of what was to
follow, and was the first model actively
to campaign in competition. Although it

*The raised hood on the SS I Tourer did little
to improve the Lyons' line (N. Baldwin)*

did not immediately win any major rewards, nevertheless the car did not disgrace itself. Henlys, the SS distributors for southern England, as they had been since Swallow days, waxed lyrical in their advertisements, stating, 'Just as the SS I Saloon has swept the country, soon this long, low, sleek open sports SS will be conspicuous on the roads everywhere'. At £325 for the 16 hp model and £335 for the 20 hp, the cars could not be said to be over costly.

Mechanically they were identical to the Coupés, and bodily they were very similar. Apart from the obvious alterations to make the cars open ones, the door tops were curved down for elbow resting and the scuttle top had a raised lip to deflect the slipstream when the folding windscreen was flat. The rear end sloped away with the spare wheel mounted at a rake where the luggage locker normally resided.

For the 1934 season yet another model was added to complement the range. This was a four-light saloon. A more genuine four-seater with the provision of rear side windows meant that the back seat passengers could at last see out. Because the saloon looked a more practical car, it appealed to the more conservative members of the motoring public. Mechanically it was identical to the Coupé and the Tourer. But that year the whole range underwent various changes. Engine sizes were increased to 2143 cc and 2663 cc, and the track was enlarged a further two inches to 4 ft 5 in. A stronger cruciform-braced frame allowed rear passengers more leg room, and the four-speed gearbox inherited synchromesh on second, third and fourth gears. Further improvements included self-cancelling trafficators (these had been an optional extra), Silentblock spring shackles, quick-action filler cap and reversing lamps, to say nothing of the chrome-plated band to the spare wheel cover. The most noticeable exterior change was the acquisition of a new and more imposing radiator without the previous bisecting slat. The hexagonal SS badge appeared on the exterior for the first time, mounted on this new revised radiator.

The SS II which, apart from the addition of a four-speed gearbox, had remained unchanged since its introduction, benefited in late 1933 from major revision and updating. Most importantly, the SS II was now provided with a specially designed low-built chassis along the lines of the SS I, with the wheelbase increased from 7 ft 5½ in to 8 ft 8 in, and the track by 1½ in to 3 ft 10½ in. This had the effect of making

what was previously a very cramped little car into a small four-seater. The original cycle wings were discarded, to be replaced by the same flowing style of 'big sister'.

A Saloon supplemented the range. This was like the SS I, a Coupé restyled with rear side windows, and it made a very pleasant and popular small car. In 1935 these two styles were joined by a third when the SS II Tourer was announced.

When it came to engines for the SS IIs, you could choose either Standard's 10 hp or their 12 hp, and they would have cost you £260 and £265 respectively for the Coupé and Saloon, plus a further £5 if you chose the larger engine.

In late 1934, William Walmsley, who did not have Lyons's ambition, resigned from the company and involved himself

in the manufacture of one of his hobb namely, caravans.

The company was by now produc a range of five models (soon to increased), with an output of 1,800 c a year from a factory site that had b expanded to some 13 acres. Once m it changed its name, this time to SS C Ltd, and was floated as a public comp late in 1935, raising some £85,000. I interesting to note that profits w approximately doubling each year, w £12,000 for 1931/2, £22,000 for 1932 and £37,000 for 1933/4.

Around this period more attent began to be given to the mechan attributes necessary if SS were to m further progress. While the style of th products had achieved wide accla they had suffered from jibes such 'more show than go', highlighting fact that the cars' performance bar

24

ved up to the promise evoked by their porting body designs. Just as Lyons had hieved independence of design by having his own chassis frames, so he wanted move a step nearer complete dependence regarding the power unit. These desires led to two major pernalities appearing on the SS stage. irstly, Lyons consulted and contracted ith Harry Weslake, who was building reputation for his work with carburaon and cylinder-head gasflow and sign. Secondly, it was decided that the ne had come for a proper engineering epartment to be set up. William eynes, at 32, was appointed chief gineer, and he was to assume an portance in succeeding years second ly to Lyons himself. After an apprenceship with Humber, he was singled t and seconded to the design office here he soon found himself in charge

of the Stress Office. When Lyons was looking for a suitable man to set up his engineering department, Grinham and Dawtry, who were in charge of design at Standard and had been Heynes's bosses at Humber, suggested the young man who had so impressed them. The task facing Heynes at SS was formidable. A new chassis had to be designed for the completely new model scheduled to be announced in five months' time.

In announcing the 1935 range, a further body style became available on the SS I chassis, this being an attractive Airline body. Company advertising proclaimed: 'The Airline Saloon – acclaimed from the moment of its introduction as the most beautiful interpretation of streamlining. This model is characterized by a modernity of outline, dignified in its restraint'. This style, in vogue at the time, featured a rounded tail

incorporating a large boot, twin-mounted spare wheels in painted covers on either front wing, and very rakish horizontal bonnet louvres. Sadly, the model did not seem to catch on, which ironically accentuates its desirability today.

The year 1935 saw several mechanical improvements incorporated in the whole range. These consisted of a new high-compression head (Harry Weslake having advised here), bigger sump, higher lift camshaft and twin RAG carburet-

1 *An SS I Tourer supplied by P. J. Evans, one of the company's first agents (Mrs J. B. Parker)* 2 *The much revised and lengthened SS II, in saloon form, made the car rather less distinguishable from its larger stablemate* 3 *A representative of the Bolton constabulary receives their first SS II Tourer in 1935 (J C)*

tors. The catalogue for that year listed metallic colour schemes for £5 extra. For the same amount, DWS four-wheel permanent jacks could be supplied, provided they were specified at the time of ordering. A period Philco car radio would cost rather more, at 16 guineas.

In March 1935, SS introduced the SS I Drophead Coupé. Mechanically identical to the Coupé, it also looked very similar but this time the 'pram irons' to the roof were no dummies but actually hinged the hood. This ingeniously folded down out of sight below a hinged cover, leaving only the closed 'pram irons' visible. To complete the effect, the window frames could be removed and stowed in the rear compartment.

Just 105 of these dropheads were built. They were priced at £380 for the 16 hp version or £5 more for the 20 hp car.

Also introduced in March 1933 was the new SS 90 sports car. This was fitted with the 2.7-litre side-valve engine and a close ratio gearbox. The prototype had a rounded tail with the spare wheel mounted into a recess. However, the production versions had what was, for the period, the almost obligatory slab tank rear end, with the spare wheel mounted vertically. The basis was an SS I chassis shortened by some 1 ft 3 in and fitted with André Telecontrol shock absorbers. As the name implies, the to

1

2

3

eed was reputed to be 90 mph, and for at privilege you would have to pay a odest £395. The SS 90, of which only including the prototype were built, s quickly overshadowed by the S 100, due to be announced in only a w months' time.

Lyons took an SS 90 to an SS Car ub weekend event at Blackpool and, hough not officially competing, monstrated the new car over a speed st course on the sea front to record a time that was nearly seven seconds quicker than the fastest official competitor. His pleasure at this must have been somewhat lessened when he heard that the secretary of the club had absconded with the club funds, leaving Lyons to settle the not inconsiderable hotel bill.

1 *With the adoption of a new Swallow-designed chassis, the enlarged SS II Coupé became a full four-seater* (Mrs Bayne) 2 *The SS Airline was certainly a departure from normal Lyons thinking, and the last time he was to allow fashion to dictate to him* 3, 4 *The SS I Drophead Coupé : the final manifestation of the SS I line and surely the happiest, with its beautiful folding 'wig top'.* (National Motor Museum; J C) 5 *The SS 90 : a beautifully blended design but as yet without the power to match the expectation suggested by the style* (J C)

3 THE SS JAGUAR

The name Jaguar made its first appearance on new models that were more sober in style, more akin to the Bentleys and similar cars of the period, but gained much in practicability. Competitive pricing ensured value-for-money and as technical standards and methods of production improved, prosperity continued. Only the outbreak of war could temporarily arrest the company's progress.

1

JAGUAR
MASCOT

DESIGNED EXPRESSLY FOR SS
CARS LTD~MANUFACTURERS
OF THE JAGUAR CAR~BY THE
EMINENT ARTIST & SCULPTOR:

J. Gordon-Crosby

PRICE TWO GUINEAS

2

3

4

e year 1935 brought a new range and ew name, for these new models were be known as SS Jaguars. At first ended only as a model name to be lied to the two new saloons and the 100 sports car announced in September of the same year, the name of Jaguar uired greater significance as time passed. This significance was so great that e of the major English dictionaries ines the word as 'jaguar (jagew-er) n. ge yellowish spotted carnivorous mal of cat family; (tr) (cap) make of werful motorcars'. It appears to be the only make of car to be accorded this compliment because the only other car names to be listed, such as rover, morris and triumph have merely their traditional definitions noted.

The new name was chosen after the Nelson Advertising Agency had prepared a list of birds, fishes and mammals for Lyons. He had no hesitation in choosing Jaguar with its allusions to excitement and speed, and the memories it held for him of stories he had been told about the Jaguar aero engine.

The publicity department was soon at work glorifying the new models. 'The car of the future has arrived. Swift as the

1 *The 1936 SS badge, incorporating the new model name of Jaguar (* J C *)* 2 *An early advertisement for the famous mascot that has come to be known as 'the leaping Jaguar' (* J C *)* 3 *An SS Jaguar 2½ ohv saloon at rest with Eastnor Castle in the background (* National Motor Museum *)* 4 *A period shot of the 2½ saloon showing its touring capabilities (* Mrs E. Nicholson *)* 5 *The splendidly proportioned lines of the 2½ ohv tourer, photographed in California*

wind – silent as a shadow come the SS Jaguars', claimed a lavish six-page pull-out advertising feature in the *Autocar* of 18th October 1935. 'Effortless speed combined with perfect Town "manners", make driving a sheer delight'.

The new SS Jaguar saloons were endowed with a completely new Lyons-designed body. For the first time, the company offered four doors and this, plus the better proportioned shape, made for a less dramatic appearance but more practical and comfortable accommodation. It had the usual Lyons style, and indeed the shape was a step nearer to the contemporary Bentley, which cost nearly four times as much. Lyons, with his flair for the dramatic, arranged a special lunch a little before the model's announcement at the 1935 Motor Show. Those present were then asked to estimate the price of the new car. The average guess was £632. The actual price as listed was a mere £395.

Weslake had contracted to extract a minimum 95 hp from the 2½-litre, which yielded 75 hp at that time. His plan was for an overhead valve configuration, so he designed a new cylinder head with pushrod-operated overhead valves and reshaped ports and combustion chambers. The results to everyone's satisfaction, was an output not of 95 hp but of 105 hp. Furthermore, Lyons managed to persuade Standards to acquire the machinery to produce these new heads, thereby saving SS the vast capital outlay necessary had they been forced to produce them themselves. The completely new Heynes-designed box section, cruciform-braced chassis frame was no longer of Standard manufacture but was made by Rubery Owen.

Lyons had now succeeded in producing a practical saloon with style and performance, and all at a price that his competition could barely approach, let alone match.

Announced concurrently with the saloon was a tourer body, which was also fitted with the 2½-litre OHV engine in the new chassis. The combination of the lively new power unit and the stylish traditional SS open four-seater bodywork must have made for a very pleasant motor. However, not a great many were made in the two years that they were listed, and they may have been overshadowed by the new two-seater sports car.

The tourer was very similar in external appearance to the earlier SS I Tourer, with the exception of the new chromium-plated radiator grille of the saloons. And if you looked very closely you might also notice the larger 15-inch Girling brake drums and, of course, the Jaguar badge.

About that time Bill Rankin, who was head of publicity, designed the famous leaping Jaguar mascot which, with some minor revision by the famous artist F. Gordon Crosby, has become closely associated with the marque. Contrary to popular opinion, this was an optional extra, and not fitted as standard until 1957.

Alongside the 2½-litre models there was a 1½-litre version. Similar in external appearance to the larger-engined version, this model retained the old si valve engine, which meant that th cars were sadly lacking in performa compared with say, the MG of period. However, at just £285 t offered remarkable value for money ever, and were very well appreciat Both the new SS Jaguar saloons side-mounted spare wheels, the 1½-li being recognizable, apart from shorter front wings and bonnet, by top of the spare wheel casing protrud just above the bonnet line.

The 1937 brochure stated, a li hypocritically, 'Self-praise is no reco

1

idation', and proceeded to print the owing :

Capt Sir Malcolm Campbell
169 Piccadilly
London W1

r Sirs,
was so impressed with the styling quali-
of the new SS Jaguar that I decided to
one myself and you will be interested to
that I have in consequence placed an
r with your London agents, Messrs
lys Ltd
Vishing your company continued success,
Yours very truly,
M. Campbell

Pre-empted by just six months by the SS 90, the SS Jaguar 100 (to give the car its full name, although today it is more usually known as the SS 100) was announced with the saloons and tourer in September 1935. Visually very similar to the SS 90, the 100 can be identified by its slightly slanting fuel tank and spare wheel, whereas these were dead vertical on the earlier model. More minor differences included the head-lamp tie-bar, which had 100 cast into it instead of 90, different headlamps, and subtle changes to the radiator shell which had, as in all models, the winged SS emblem above the name *Jaguar*.

The chassis followed earlier SS lines but with later suspension and steering, and had a wheelbase of 8 ft 8 in. The

1 *Considered by some at the time to be too flam-boyant, the SS 100 is now thought by many to be the epitome of prewar sports car design (J C)* 2 *The spare wheel clearly protrudes above the bonnet line, distinguishing the $1\frac{1}{2}$ sv saloon (National Motor Museum)* 3 *The most famous product of the company's prewar era : the SS Jaguar 100 (Mrs E. Simms)* 4 *One hundred miles an hour indeed ! What will these young 'uns be up to next ? (Mrs E. Simms)*

4

price for the SS 100 two-seater 2663 cc sports car was just £395, for which you had a car capable of 95 mph with a 0–60 mph time of around 13 seconds. A company advertisement claimed that the model, 'though primarily for competition work, is sufficiently tractable for use as a fast tourer without modification'.

For many, the 100 was the climax of Lyons's prewar designs. It was beautifully proportioned with gracefully flowing lines that imbued the car with a sporty feel. It also gained genuine sporting success, attracting attention in Europe – testimony to the fact that the performance was beginning to match the promise.

A large number of small changes were made to the saloons and tourer in 1937. Externally the 2½-litre acquired quarterlights, P100 headlamps and faired-in sidelights. The tourer was fitted with P100s and the 1½ had the quarterlights. All models featured a re-organized interior, resulting in more comfort with greater leg room.

Late in 1937 there was further progress when a new range of models was announced to replace the 1½-litre sidevalve saloon and 2½-litre ohv saloon and tourer. The new range, offered in 1½, 2½, and 3½-litre forms with either a saloon body or drophead coupé style, were now of all-steel construction. The former method of construction, whereby steel panels were attached to a wooden frame, was superseded, and the use of wood was dropped. This new method allowed production to be increased, with the result that the total output approached 100 cars per week during 1938. But this transition to all-steel construction was not achieved without considerable trauma. Thousands of pressed panels were bought in from several suppliers, but when SS attempted to assemble them they just did not marry up. As a result, the factory stood virtually idle for several months while the situation was resolved, and so serious was the situation that bankruptcy became a possibility. Happily, everything was eventually sorted out and the new methods allowed production to be increased dramatically. This resulted in a certain trading loss being transformed into a respectable profit.

Heynes designed a new chassis for the all-steel range. Keeping abreast of the then current thinking, this consisted of 6-inch-deep side members of box section with three box-section cross members. The greater stiffness achieved obviously aided the ride of the new range. All three saloons shared the same body, which closely resembled the previous 2½ with

some subtle changes. The spare wheel disappeared from the wing, and was attached at first to the boot lid and later to a tray under the boot floor. The new bodies were somewhat larger with improved interior space and better access through larger doors.

The 1½ now had a wheelbase of 9 ft 4½ in, as opposed to the larger-engined cars with a wheelbase of 10 ft. This difference was achieved by a correspondingly reduced bonnet and 'cut-and-shut' chassis for the smallest vers[...]

The 2½-litre engine remained s[...] stantially unchanged apart fr[...] improvements to its breathing arran[...]ments, with the provision of a t[...] branch exhaust manifold. The 3½-[...] was offered with a new engine. It wa[...] principle just a larger version of the [...] litre, still basically Standard but with[...] Weslake-designed head and ot[...] refining by Heynes. With a bore [...] stroke of 82 × 110 mm, Twin SU [...]

1

rettors and two triple-branch exhaust manifolds, this new unit gave around bhp at 4500 rpm.

Country Life, in reviewing the new model, stated that 'the 3½-litre Jaguar is very remarkable car indeed and may be nestly ranked among the high-class high-performance cars of the world. . . . one had not looked at the catalogue fore trying it out, one would be given for thinking it was at least in the ,000 class.'

All three models were also offered in the attractive drophead coupé form. A well designed hood meant that the shape was pleasing whether the hood was raised or lowered.

The price of £298 was modest for the 1½-litre, but then so was the performance, with such a large, heavy body and relatively small engine. However, the luxurious appointments perhaps compensated for the lack of zest. In contrast, the 3½ litre, with its power output of

125 bhp, ensured lively performance, and a price of £465 for the drophead coupé must have made this a most attractive model in more senses than one.

1 *This shot shows the flowing Lyons lines, but here with an unusual positioning of the number plate and rear lamp (J C)* **2, 3** *The SS 100's hood was obviously a necessity rather than a styling feature (J C), whilst its dashboard was a delight to the eye (Mrs E. Simms)*

It was only logical to fit the new big engine to the 100, especially as it now had a greater chance of attaining its sporting aspirations. The 3½'s healthy output, combined with the lightness of the sports body, gave a very lively performance indeed for the period. The 'ton' was just possible, and 60 mph could be reached in a shade under 10½ seconds.

At a price of £445 there was nothing to touch the 100 for its combination of performance and price, to say nothing of its simple good looks. In other departments the SS 100 was also rated highly. The brakes were particularly good, and the roadholding inspired confidence. But the car did not escape criticism entirely. Tom Wisdom commented that 'the main fault of the SS 100, even in 2½-litre form, was that it had too much power for its rather flexible chassis. The springing, in the sports car fashion of its day, was as light as all Hell, so instead of absorbing bumps it just ricochetted the car from one bump to the next. the front anything over half an inch suspension movement brought bump stops into play'. Yet, he went to say that in spite of the magazine testers' disbelieving the performa figures at first (such was the accel tion), nevertheless the SS was 'a b liantly docile and flexible car'.

With all the new development wo is not surprising that Heynes was h pressed and began to search for

1

2

rienced man to assist him. Writing 1970, Tom Wisdom stated, 'At my gestion "Wally" Hassan, famous for work on various Thomson and lor specials, including the record-aking Hassan Special, and also on the A project in its formative stages, was ed away from Thomson and Taylor Brooklands and onto the SS payroll. e his outstanding qualities as an ineer found good scope in the elopment of the bigger, 3½-litre

SS 100 which came onto the market in late 1937.' Hassan joined the company in late 1938 with the title of Chief Experimental Engineer.

Apart from the current models, another model, most striking in appearance, graced stand No 126 at Earls Court in 1938. Lyons had designed a closed coupé body to clothe a normal 100 chassis and the result was an interesting hint of things to come. The show car had the 3½-litre engine and was priced at £595. Addi-

tionally, a 2½-litre was listed at £545 but was never produced, because only the one coupé was ever built. It had a four-

speed synchromesh gearbox giving ratios of 3-8, 4-58, 7-06 and 12-04 to 1, and the car weighed 25 cwt.

Consideration was given to comfort and there was said to be more elbow room than one might suppose. There was a large space for luggage at the back, with the rear parcel shelf opening to a horizontal position to increase carrying capacity. This same flap contained the tools in a 'well-designed tray'. The rear wings were faired inwards at the rear to reduce 'windage', and the spare wheel was carried in the tail. Side lamps were faired into the front wings, and Lucas P100s completed the front lighting equipment.

The subsequent owner who received the car as a 17th birthday present found it not altogether practical. Apparently, some modifications had to be carried out to the interior to make it drivable, the doors dropped, the small sunshine roof created a whirlwind effect, and the red colouring on the steering wheel rubbed off on the driver's trousers! But, in spite of the practical problems, the model's significance in the evolution of the company's designs cannot be overstressed.

As stated earlier, sidecar production, although inevitably overshadowed the more glamorous cars, neverthe continued apace. With the floating of Cars Ltd, Lyons had formed a separ company, Swallow Coachbuilding (1935) Ltd, with a capital of £10,000 carry on the manufacture of sideca The 1938 catalogue listed no fewer t 12 models plus the Special Swall Chassis at £8 15s 0d (less tyre and tub

Leafing through the catalogue, find the Syston Sports at £17 19s 6d; Sports Touring Coupé de Luxe w quick-lift hood operated by passen from inside; the Hurlingham Ad

1

o-seater 'evolved as a direct result of numerous enquiries we have received for a two-seater sidecar'; the Kenilworth Coupé 'which will make a direct appeal to the family man who is desirous of accommodating both passengers under cover'; the De Luxe Touring model with fashionable Vauxhall-like styling and 'constructed on the pressed steel principle'; the Tourer De Luxe, as above but with 'a dickey-seat at the rear capable of carrying a normal-sized youth up to fourteen years of age'; the Standard Launch, which looked as though it should be on water rather than on land; and the De Luxe Launch, which with its added deck rails looked like a streamlined coffin. Still turning the pages, we find the Aero Launch Coupé, the coffin with a hard-top; the Sun Saloon, a fastback coffin; the very rakish Donington Special for sporting events; and finally, at £31 10s 0d, the Ranelagh Saloon, 'the finest sidecar obtainable'.

After a couple of years of 'all-steel' production, World War II intervened and car production was phased out, although the public was destined to see the saloons and drophead coupés again after an interval of some six years.

1 *By folding back the cant rails you could easily assume the Coupe de Ville guise of the three-position hood (*National Motor Museum*)* 2 *The very beautiful if not entirely practical one-off SS 100 Coupé, as shown at the 1938 Motor Show (*The Motor*)* 3 *The frontal aspect, although cluttered by later badges and horns, gives a hint of things to come (*J C*)* 4 *In parallel with the saloons, the sidecar range by the late 1930s showed more subtlety of line (*J C*)*

4 THE WAR AND AFTER

Aircraft repair and sub-contract work kept the factories busy during the war and the new machinery introduced and techniques learnt were to be of future benefit. The early post-war period was a dull time devoid of new models but it was also a period of consolidation with exciting projects at an embryonic stage. The company was becoming increasingly more independent, particularly of Standards, and much more of a complete manufacturer.

1

wards the end of 1939, war work was commenced and car production gradually faded out. In comparison with the rest of Coventry, the Jaguar factory escaped serious bomb damage, although in late 1940 six workshops were destroyed. Apart from some experimental work, the company increased production of the old faithful sidecars for military use, supplying them to the RAF, the Admiralty, the Army and the National Fire Service; carried out a variety of aircraft production and repair work; and produced some 700 trailers of various kinds per week.

The aircraft work included the repair of Whitley bombers and later, of Wellingtons; the manufacture of various tooling; the production of wings, frames and bomb doors for Short Stirling bombers, Avro Lancasters, Spitfires, and de Havilland Mosquitos; and parts for the Cheetah seven-cylinder radial engine. Towards the end of the war the company was instructed to manufacture the complete centre sections for the then highly secret Gloster Meteor III jet fighter.

Other work included lightweight trailers to be towed behind motorcycles and jeeps, a folding sidecar, mule carts for the Burma campaign, and two lightweight jeep-type vehicles. The last-named were designated the VA and VB, and were intended for parachute dropping. The VA had a V-twin JAP engine

1 *Armstrong Whitworth Whitley bombers: some 80 sets of wings were modified by SS cars to carry heavier bombs* (J C) 2 *Ironically the war took SS back to where it all began, with the major emphasis placed on sidecars instead of cars* (J C) 3 *SS fitters working on the reduction gear of an Armstrong Whitworth Whitley bomber* (J C) 4 *The disciplines of war were much in evidence here* (J C)

ANY PERSON who has scrapped a detail part, and to hide this, fabricates a similar part from unapproved material, will be assumed to have committed an act of sabotage and proceedings will be taken accordingly.

SS CARS LIMITED

but, because this was not considered powerful enough, the VB was built with a Ford 10 unit. What is particularly interesting about these vehicles is that they were of unitary construction – a method used for Jaguar's production cars some years later, and they were independently sprung all round, again preceding the production cars by approximately 20 years. But these vehicles never proceeded beyond the prototype stage, because by the time they were sufficiently developed, aircraft were capable of carrying the larger, more conventional jeeps.

The war had both bad and good effects on the company's progress. Lyons, having made record profits of £60,000 in 1938/9, had purchased one of SS's panel suppliers – Motor Panels – with a view to becoming independent of outside sources in this major sphere. But because it was starved of profits, the company did not have the money to recommence car production and reluctantly sold Motor Panels to Rubery Owen in order to finance postwar production.

However, one important benefit of the war work was the breadth of experie gained and the extra machin acquired. The experience of airc manufacture and technique was manifest itself later, particularly in field of competition.

With hostilities drawing to a cl thoughts returned to car producti New models were planned, but v steel shortages, rationing, and ot problems, it was thought best to introduce the prewar models as a s gap.

At an extraordinary general meet

1

2

3

March 1945, it was decided to change the company name because the initials SS had by that time acquired an unhappy connotation with the Nazis' use of this title. So the company acquired the name of Jaguar Cars. This was a name that was to become increasingly familiar across the Atlantic, because Lyons had realized the value of that potential market and was beginning to exploit it.

At home, however, with austerity at its worst, you had to wait anything up to eight years for a new Jaguar.

The sidecar business was sold to the Helliwell Group, who in turn sold it to Tube Investments. This company produced, alongside the sidecar range, the Swallow Gadabout – a 125 cc scooter – and the Swallow Doretti sports car, based on the Triumph TR2. In 1956 TI sold the Swallow Coachbuilding Co (1935) Ltd to Watsonian of Birmingham.

1 Close on 100 Gloster Meteor III centre sections were built in the later stages of the war

(J C) **2** *VA jeep: SS began to apply the construction methods learnt from aircraft to the lightweight jeeps for parachute dropping, developed for the War Department* (J C) **3** *VB jeep: a variation on the theme but with more power, provided by a Ford 10 side-valve engine – note the interesting tyre pattern* (J C) **4** *Immediate postwar restrictions dictated the reintroduction of the prewar range, but postwar austerity did not preclude traditional opulence. The thinner chrome band, seen here on a 1½-litre, was one of the few features that distinguished it from the prewar versions* (J C) **5** *The Jaguar window transfer shows that this 2½-litre is a postwar model* (J C)

Shortly before the end of the war, Jaguar's took another step forward by acquiring from the Standard Motor Company all the machinery used in the manufacture of the 2½- and 3½-litre engines. This ensured the company's independence and, with hindsight, was viewed with regret by Captain Black of Standard's.

This early postwar period was a difficult one for every firm – not least for Jaguar. It was an era of strikes, power cuts, steel shortages, coal shortages, and so on. As stated, the prewar models were re-introduced in mid-1945, in almost identical form. The 1½-litre was supplemented by a 1½-litre special equipment model, which had been available just prior to the war. It had a heater, better headlamps, adjustable front seats, foglamps and a 'specially finished luggage locker'. The only visible distinguishing features between pre- and post-war cars were a rather thinner waist band on the latter models, plus differe[nt] badges and the word *Jaguar* replaci[ng] the SS on the wheel spinners.

The 2½-litre and 3½-litre models we[re] also re-introduced in mid-1945. T[he] only under-the-skin changes from th[e] prewar counterparts were as follows. Metalistik crankshaft torsion[al] vibrational damper was incorporated, [there] were Girling 2LS brakes, and a hyp[oid] final drive for both models. The revis[ed] final drive was also fitted to the 1½-litr[e]

At that time, with exports assuming immense importance (particularly to the American market), the 3½-litre was especially popular. The Americans were used to big engines and fuel consumption bothered them little; whereas in Britain, with petrol rationing in operation, the thirst of the 3½ was unacceptable, and the 1½, despite its lack of performance, was preferred for its thrifty consumption.

Company advertising claimed that 'every Jaguar is a full five-seater car of high performance, luxuriously appointed with that impeccable finish which for years has been associated with the name Jaguar'. They now felt able to call it 'The Finest Car of its Class in the World'.

1 A gentleman of the constabulary appears to be having some difficulty in entering this 1½-litre (J C) 2 The 3½-litre Jaguar, a rare sight in car-starved Britain in the late 1940s when the home market took second place to export (Mrs E. Nicholson) 3 Proving that nothing is new, a team of ex-servicemen, having formed a rural travelling maintenance team, service a market gardener's 3½-litre in Worcestershire 4 The 1½, 2½ and 3½ litre models were produced as a drophead and most were exported. 5 Superb styling, but not for claustrophobic rear seat passengers (National Motor Museum) 6 The Mark V – successful stopgap between prewar continuation and postwar innovation (J C)

6

The drophead coupés were again offered from December 1947, and the vast majority of these were exported. Another important overseas market for Jaguar products, perhaps second only to the United States, was Belgium.

The Belgian Jaguar distributor, a Madame Bourgeois of Brussels – an ebullient character by all accounts – was also an energetic and fervent propagator of the Jaguar cause. Sales flourished – so much so that the Belgian Government banned the importing of all cars costing more than £600. Lyons replied by arranging for his cars to be assembled at the Vanden Plas works in Belgium. This had the added result of making the Jaguars more competitive in price. The Belgians dropped the ban in 1949, the factory closed and the production of mainly drophead models ceased.

In September 1948 the company announced its first new postwar model, although it was actually another stopgap compromise. This model was named the Mark V, for no better reason than that the production car was the fifth prototype to be built.

Standard's had stopped production of the 1½-litre engine so the new Mark V was available in just 2½ and 3½-litre for A new chassis was introduced whic according to the company's brochure lavish production with individua affixed colour illustrations rather li giant cigarette cards), was 'scientifica designed and, for its weight is probab the most rigid frame incorporated in a passenger car'. The stiffness of t frame contributed to the Mark V's go roadholding and ride. The adoption 16-inch rather than 18-inch diamet wheels reduced the centre of gravity a improved the car's appearance. A new developed 6.7 section Dunlop ty

1

2

3

roved grip and comfort.

Most significantly, the car featured [ind]ependent front wheel suspension, [whi]ch had been originally designed in [193]8 and continually tested and [dev]eloped since that date. It worked on [the] torsion bar principle first developed [by] Citröen and long favoured by [Ha]ynes, who gradually developed it into [a ve]ry neat system.

[T]he new Mark V could be had in [drop]head coupé form although this [origi]nal is extremely scarce in Britain [bec]ause the vast majority, like the earlier [mo]dels (sometimes unofficially referred

to as Mk IVs), were exported, mainly across the Atlantic.

Like its predecessors, the new car had a three-position hood – fully raised, coupe-de-ville (open over the front seats only) and fully open. In any of these positions the model looked elegant and the car-starved British public must have been extremely envious of those in other countries who were given precedence at that time. The Mark Vs were tough, reliable souls if not terribly exciting, but excitement aplenty was just around the corner.

1 The Mark V continued Jaguar's association with the police, as an envious public waited for its new Jaguar (J C) 2 Two-toning suited the Mark V, the first production Jaguar to carry spot lamps 3 The Mark V's interior – British tradition at its best—oozing luxury (J C) 4 The contrasting curious coachwork in the background illustrates the traditional line of this export Mark V (National Motor Museum) 5 The Mark V Drophead, still stylish but a little less happy with the spat, which contributed to the general heaviness of the rear (J C)

5

5 THE XK ENGINE

The introduction of the famous new engine was to be the most significant step forward yet and helped guide the fortunes of the company right into the 1980s. In a period of austerity, when 'export or die' was the dictum, the new Jaguar sports cars and saloons brought a sense of pride to the British, doing much for international prestige, reinforced by patriotic competitive success.

far back as 1939, a new engine had
[be]en planned by Lyons and chief
[eng]ineer Heynes, but the war intervened
[and], although they discussed ideas dur-
[ing] fire-watching at the factory, the
[act]ual design was not laid down by
[He]ynes and his team, Wally Hassan and
[Cl]aude Bailey, until 1946. They were
[giv]en an entirely free hand in the design,
[ha]ving to produce an engine with a
[m]inimum output of 160 bhp, extreme
[sm]oothness and flexibility, a capacity for
[co]ntinuous development and, interest-
[ing]ly, Lyons specified that the engine
[mu]st be a 'glamorous' one in the manner
[of t]he Bugatti.

That they succeeded, and almost to the
letter, is now a well known fact. The
resulting engine, named XK, is arguably
the greatest and certainly the most ver-
satile ever produced. It proceeded to
power exciting production sports cars,
Le Mans winners, a variety of saloons in
the 1950s and 1960s, Scorpion tanks and
armoured cars, Dennis fire engines,
record-breaking power boats and, in the
1970s and early 1980s, silent, sophisticated executive saloons.

The XK120 was designed and built as
a publicity exercise and as a mobile
testbed for this new XK engine. The
intention was to build a limited number,

prior to the engine's being used in an
important new large saloon car to be
introduced a little later. This was the
Mark VII, duly announced in 1950. But
the acclaim and orders for the XK120
were such that the car quickly came to
be thought of as a serious production

1 *HKV 455 – a very well known number plate
seen on the first XK120 Open Two-Seater
Super Sports. Note the straight screen pillars,
which were fitted to very early cars. (*National
Motor Museum*) 2 The XK120's impact was
immeasurable, attracting attention from far
and wide, typified by these distinguished visitors
(*J C*)

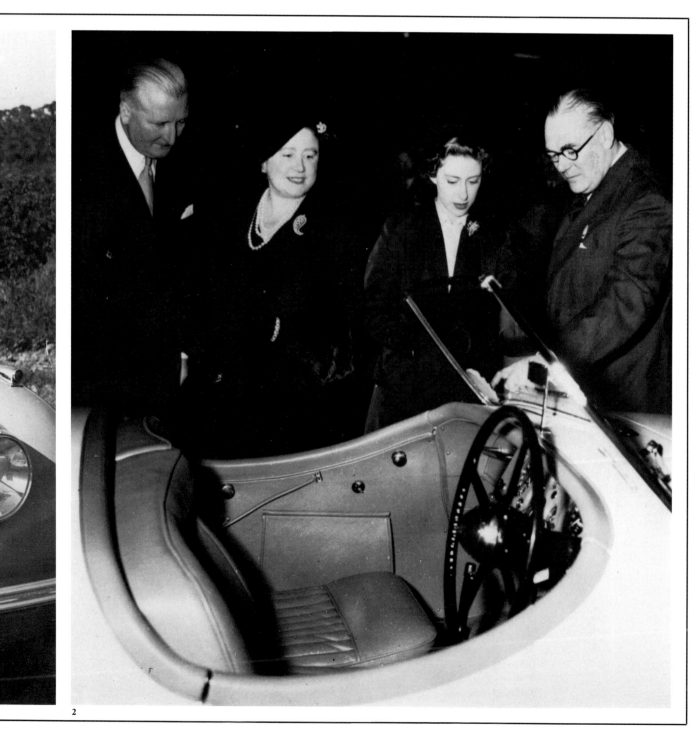

2

venture. More than 10,000 were built, most of which were exported to America.

Although Heynes, Hassan and Bailey had discussed ideas for a new engine during the war, they started in earnest to design it only in 1946. The first engine design was a four-cylinder job designated XA, X standing for experimental. However the first engine to be produced was the XF, a four-cylinder engine of 1360 cc (66.5 × 98 mm). Its crankshaft was not sufficiently strong, so next came the XG. At that time Bill Heynes was very friendly with the well known sports racing driver Leslie Johnson. Johnson had a BMW 328 which Heynes borrowed and converted one of the then current Jaguar pushrod engines to the same type of head. This XG had a capacity of $1\frac{1}{2}$ litres. The engine was installed in a BMW and Walter Hassan 'ran this car for thousands of miles', testing not only the engine but also various types of suspension, including the 'Lockhead air type'. But this engine was too noisy and was superseded by the XJ, on which basic specification the production engine was to be based. This XJ design was produced as a 2-litre, four-cylinder and a 3.2-litre, six-cylinder. The latter was found to be lacking in low speed torque, so the stroke was increased, giving the final capacity of 3442 cc. These engines, after exhaustive testing (mainly on the four-cylinder) and minor adjustments and alterations, were given the designation XK. The cylinder head with hemispherical combustion chambers and cross-flow design had been the work of Harry Weslake. On an 8:1 compression ratio the larger engine produced 160 bhp at 5,200 rpm, and it also looked right, with its polished aluminium camshaft covers. Maximum bmep was 140 lbs sq in at 2,500 rpm, and bhp per square inch of piston area produced a figure of 3,175, and peak piston speed in feet per minute was 3,360.

In the summer of 1948, before the public knew of the car that was to come, the works had lent an XJ four-cylinder engine to the well known recordbreaker, Major Goldie Gardner. He used it to good effect in his streamlined car EX 135, breaking three International Class E records with a mean speed of 176.694 mph – from just 2 litres.

The situation in 1948 was that Jaguar had no sports car currently listed, yet they had a new chassis and a brand new high performance engine. So with the 1948 Earls Court Motor Show not very far off, the decision was taken to build a sports car. There were several reasons for this. Lyons realized from the SS 100 the value of publicity resulting from suc-

cessful racing competition, resulting in a sporting image being acquired for the Jaguar company as a whole. But additionally, it was an ideal opportunity to try out and, hopefully, prove the new engine in a low-production model prior to the large-scale production envisaged when the Mark VII was announced. Furthermore, the sports car was likely to be bought by enthusiasts, who would be more tolerant of any teething problems.

The decision having been taken, it was

now up to William Lyons to spee[d] design a body. The result won almost u[ni]versal acclaim and a measure of the rig[ht]ness of this example of the Lyons lin[e] the high esteem in which the shap[e is] held today, more than 40 years later. [We] must remember that in 1948 an [en]enveloping body was virtually unhe[ard] of for a sports car, the only precede[nt] being the BMW and a few one-[offs] designed by Italian specialist coa[ch] builders. And certainly the standar[d]

1

2

fort and protection offered was
ivalled.

almost every way the XK set new
ndards – in performance, styling,
, roadholding, docility (for such a
, comfort and, above all, in value for
ney. The factory was able to claim
it was the Fastest Production Car in
World.

he chassis and suspension evolved
the Mark VII, used in the interim
rk V and slightly modified for the

sports car, consisted of two deep box
members running from the front to just
in front of the rear axle, where these
members gradually decreased in size and
swept up over the axle. The front
suspension consisted of independent
wide-based top and bottom wishbones
and long torsion bars located around the
middle of the chassis. Rear springing
was by semi-elliptics and lever-type
shock absorbers, and Lockheed full
hydraulic brakes worked in 12-inch

1 *In 1948 there was nothing on the road that
could keep up with an XK120 (National
Motor Museum)* 2 *An early steel-bodied
XK120, complete with its 'all weather' equipment (J C)* 3 *Not surprisingly the exciting
XK120 led the great Jaguar postwar export
boom, many being ordered from the USA
(National Motor Museum)* 4 *The frontal
aspect of the wings makes an interesting comparison with the prewar 100 Coupé – the
spotlamps were an extra (B. Bradnack)* 5
*Occupying the XK120's cockpit must have been
every schoolboy's dream in the early 1950s*

5

drums. The gearbox was a four-speed one with synchromesh on second, third and fourth, and the ratios were 3.64, 4.98, and 12.29 to 1, giving approximate speeds of 62 mph in second and 90 mph in third. The standard axle ratio was 3.54:1 which translated, allowing for changes in tyre radius, to 4951 rpm at 120 mph in top. Dunlop Road Speed tyres were fitted with normal pressure of 25 psi all round, but 'for fast driving when comfort is not of primary importance' they could be pumped up to 35 all round. Lucas de Luxe electrical equipment was fitted throughout with 'twin batteries with constant voltage-controlled ventilated dynamo'.

For £998 (£1298 with purchase tax) you had a car that could better 120 mph,

accelerate to 60 mph in 10 seconds, or potter gently through rush-hour London. So remarkable were the factory's claims that many of the public and indeed most journalists found that they could not believe them, dismissing them as exaggerated publicity.

Jaguar had a problem. The public and press alike needed proof in a form that was conclusive. So, a party of journalists was flown to Jabbeke motorway in Belgium, where a carriageway had been closed. The Belgian RAC had set up official timing apparatus and an XK120 with R.M.V. (Soapy) Sutton was ready and waiting.

Lofty England recently recalled, 'Soapy was a very nervous character until he got going. He used to stand there

shaking, smoking madly and dropp ash everywhere, particularly down h self! Anyway the car was got rea including tying the sidescreens to hoodsticks so they wouldn't fly off, the plane was late. There was everywhere!'

The car was a standard example w the addition of an undershield, optional extra. First run, with hood side screens in position, achie 126.448 mph. Then the windscreen detached, a small cowl replaced it ar metal tonneau was attached to cover passenger seat. This run produce speed of 132.916 mph in a north direction and 133.596 mph in southerly direction – a mean speed 132.596 mph. To conclude

1

onstration, Sutton motored past the zed journalists at 10 mph – in top

espite their incredulity, the public not been slow in placing orders for new car, and it was realized after a days of the Show that demand would iderably outstrip the 'couple of hun-l' originally envisaged. The first cars e constructed in aluminium over ash ues. Obviously this method was not ed to mass production, so it was essary to tool up for pressed steel ies. This inevitably meant long ys, and although 240 aluminium-ied cars were made, it was not until -1950 that the first steel-bodied cars e produced and that XK120s became lable in any quantity. Even then the

majority went abroad, mainly to the States and to Australia, the company's largest export markets at that time.

In 1950 William Lyons, not content solely with being President of the Society of Motor Manufacturers, again stole the show at the 35th International Motor Exhibition at Earls Court. The star on this occasion was the first entirely new Jaguar saloon to be presented since the war, the culmination of five years' research and development – the Mark VII.

As has already been mentioned, the twin-cam engine was designed and developed not for a sports car range, which was merely a convenient mobile test-bed, but for a completely new big Jaguar saloon. This model was the

Mark VII, and the XK engine gave this very large (overall length 16 ft 4½ in) and heavy (33 cwt dry) car a top speed of 100 mph and, for the period and type of car, lively acceleration, with a 0–60 mph time of 12½ seconds.

Apart from the engine, the saloon and the sports car had much in common

1 A solid-wheeled car, this XK120 is correctly fitted with spats; the separate chromed front sidelights were fitted until 1953 2 Works driver 'Soapy' Sutton preparing for his famous 132 mph run at Jabbeke (JC) 3 In 1953 Jaguar showed this XK120 MC complete with 18-carat gold-plated wire wheels (note later sidelights and front wing ventilators) (National Motor Museum) 4 The Mark VII – the start of the 'Grace, Space and Pace' era (JC)

BY APPOINTMENT
O H.M. QUEEN ELIZABETH
THE QUEEN MOTHER
TOR CAR MANUFACTURERS
JAGUAR CARS LTD

3

4

mechanically. The chassis designs were similar, being a straight plane steel box section frame of immense strength. Suspension and steering followed XK120 lines closely. The brakes, a Girling Autostatic fully hydraulic self-adjusting system, not surprisingly because of the weight of the car, had servo assistance. The standard of ride and smoothness was impressive and led Jaguar to claim that the car gave 'the impression that the engine is merely idling when the car is travelling at high cruising speeds'. After all, the engine was only revolving at a shade more than 5,000 rpm at the ton, and a piston speed of 2,500 ft min produced a top gear speed of 69 mph.

The interior, with its vast leather-covered seats (it was described as five-seater, six optional) and an almost excessive amount of walnut, positively oozed with luxury, redolent of prewar opulence. Publicity material was at pains to point out that 'four large suitcases and four big golf bags can be carried, with room still left for sundry small items of hand luggage'. The boot had a capacity of 17 cubic feet, and large cubby lockers were provided on either side of the instrument panel, one fitted with a [l] and key.

Not surprisingly, the Americ[an] immediately coveted the new salo[on] which had, after all, been designed w[ith] that market in mind. Within two or t[hree] months, orders had been taken to [a] value of approximately 30 million [dol]lars, and Lyons had a real big vol[ume] winner. This inevitably imposed p[ro]duction problems and necessitate[d a] move from Holbrook Lane to the pres[ent] Browns Lane site where one million s[q ft] of space allowed considerable expans[ion] and a resultant rise in output.

It is interesting to note that Lyons, who had tried to imitate the Rolls Royce particularly the Bentley in appearance, was now approaching them in technical specifications as well. This narrowing of the gap has continued to the present day. Incidentally, there was no Mark VI Jaguar because Bentley were already using this designation, and Jaguar's adoption of the title Mark VII precluded Bentleys from continuing their numerical progression – no doubt a source of some annoyance to them.

The XK120 Fixed-Head Coupé was introduced at the Geneva Motor Show in 1951. It was basically a roadster with a roof but to put it just like that simply does not do justice to the marriage, which was another Lyons success.

Reminiscent of prewar Bugattis, the FHC was altogether a more comfortably appointed car than its stablemate. It had wind-up windows, figured walnut fascia and door cappings, veneered instrument panel and better heating and ventilation. The performance was little different from that of the roadster, although a special equipment model was offered with $\frac{3}{4}$-inch lift camshafts, a dual exhaust system, and 8:1 compression, developing 180 bhp. These SE models also featured wire wheels, a special crankshaft damper, and stiffer 1-inch torsion

1 *In spite of its size, the new XK engine propelled the Mark VII at 100 mph (*J C*)* **2** *Interior of a Mark VII belonging to Major Goldie Gardner, the famous record-breaker, competing in a Coronation Concours d'Elegance at Brighton (*National Motor Museum*)* **3** *A Jaguar Mark VII helps to perform the opening ceremony of the new Motor Industries Research Association (MIRA) test track (*N. Dewis*)* **4** *Part of a glamorous early 1950s filmstar image: poodles and Jaguar Mark VII (*National Motor Museum*)*

bars. They were designated XK120 Ms in the States and were available in roadster form as well. Acceleration from 0–60 mph now took some 9.9 secs, and the fixed-head weighed in at some 27 cwt as opposed to 25½ cwt for the original alloy cars, and 26½ cwt for the steel roadsters. A couple of features first seen on the closed 120s were also adopted for the roadsters, namely footwell ventilators and sidelights faired into the front wings.

The Fixed Head was a Grand Touring car in the proper manner, and in right-hand drive form is a rare car today because only 195 were produced. It was stated in the factory-produced Salesman's Data Book for 1954 that the 'Special Equipment model is produced in series and is, therefore, eligible for acceptance in competitive events for production sports cars'.

Stirling Moss had an XK120 FHC with which he used to tow a caravan to meetings. When I asked him recently if he remembered it, he replied. 'I remember it very well because the caravan broke loose and smashed! But I do remember the 120. It was a very pretty car and in its time handled quite well. It was a very good long-legged car. Suited me well.'

The design and construction of the C-Type is covered in the competition section, because the C-Type was designed purely with competition in mind – hence its original title of XK120C, the C standing for competition.

First raced in earnest in June 1951, the factory offered a 'production' version in August of the following year. This was to allow private owners, particularly across the Atlantic, to compete against the sports racing Ferraris, etc, on equal terms.

The C makes an extremely good road car as I can testify, having had on one occasion to try and keep up with an extremely rapidly driven D-Type along country roads. Yet the car is docile

1 *Jaguar show stand*, circa 1953, featuring the Le Mans winning C-Type, XK120 Roadster, XK120 DHC and Mark VII (J C) **2** Not so much a racing machine like its open sister, the 120 FHC admirably suited the man with sporting aspirations at the weekend (National Motor Museum) **3** The C-Type made a fine road machine, and this example was obviously used as such, judging by the tax disc and registration number (National Motor Museum) **4** With its added sophistication and comfort, the XK120 Fixed-Head made a good, fast, long-distance touring car (J C) **5** The C-Type belonged to the era when competing cars could be and were driven to events such as Le Mans (N. Dewis)

5

Announced at the Geneva Show in 1951 and seen here at Earls Court the same year, the breathtakingly beautiful Fixed-Head XK120

1

2

3

4

enough to trundle through towns, although there is not much space for the shopping.

Including the works cars, 53 C-Types in all were produced. The production version cost just £2,327, including purchase tax of £832. There were no fundamental differences between these cars and the one which had won Le Mans in 1951. With road use in mind, some concession was made to creature comforts with basic trimming of the cockpit. Also, a horn was required by law, a law that permitted the 140 mph plus of which the C-Type was capable. There was no other car in production (even though production was limited) at that time capable of keeping up with a well-driven C-Type.

Of the 53 C-Types that were built, all but about half-a-dozen were production Cs, but irrespective of whether they were works cars or not, they were numbered in the sequence XKC 001 to XKC 053.

Introduced in April 1953, the XK 120 Drophead Coupé was a compromise between the out-and-out sporting Roadster and the more sophisticated Fixed Head. Its mechanics were the same as those of the other models, but it was fitted with a lined, folding 'first quality padded mohair' hood, with an interior light and a rear window that could be unzipped. Interior trim was similar to that of the more refined Fixed Head. The result was a pleasant and practical car that looked attractive with the hood up. But it was a little spoilt by the bulky folded hood, which left rather a pronounced bulge to the line, just behind the doors. This model is the rarest of all the XKs, because only 1,765 were produced, compared with 2,678 Fixed Heads and 7,612 Roadsters.

The colours available for the XK range of coachwork at that time were as follows: Suede Green, Cream, Birch Grey, Battleship Grey, Lavender Grey, Black, Pastel Green, Pastel Blue, Dove Grey, British Racing Green and Red.

1 *The XK120 Drophead Coupé announced in 1953 completed the trio, with most of the Fixed Head's comforts but still with the option of open-air motoring* (J C) 2 *Apart from the C-Type, the entire range for 1953 was on display in the Birmingham showrooms of P. J. Evans, still today one of Jaguar's major distributors* (R. Gore) 3 *Concours events featuring car and owner were a popular pastime in the 1950s and here is an unusual two-toned XK120 DHC* (National Motor Museum) 4 *A mouth-watering display of Jaguar's products, including a lone C-Type, awaiting despatch. All but a handful are left-hand drive* (J C)

With no less than four greys listed they sound almost dull compared with the Swallow colour schemes.

It is interesting to note in this day of increased awareness of fuel consumption, that an XK120 competing in the 1954 Cheltenham Motor Club Economy Run achieved the remarkable figure of 58.7 mpg.

At the beginning of 1953 the Americans were courted yet again with the introduction for the Mark VIIs of an optional automatic transmission that would not be available on the home market for a couple of years. This was followed in 1954 by the further option of Laycock de Normanville electrically selected overdrive on the manual models.

During the previous year Norman Dewis, Jaguar's chief tester, had taken several cars over to Jabbeke in Belgium, including a Mark VII, with which he managed to record a mean speed of 121.7 mph.

At the 1954 Motor Show, coinciding with the introduction of the XK140s with the uprated 190 bhp engine, was the revised Mark VIIM, which utilized the same engine together with stiffer suspension and closer gear ratio. Externally only minor differences we evident, with Le Mans type headlam foglamps moved to the extremities of t bumpers and replaced by horn grill altered bumpers without the mid shallow rib, and the previo semaphore-type indicators giving way the later flashing type. To combat bo roll the torsion bars were increased diameter from $\frac{15}{16}$ in to 1 in. Inside, t pointed horn push first seen in t XK120 was changed to the flat, a safer, XK140 type.

The D-Type, the most famous

ar's sports racing cars and arguably
most famous postwar sports racing
of all, was made available on a limited
duction basis from the middle of
5.

he construction and specification of
D-Type is covered in the competi-
section, but suffice it to say here
t by this time the works D-Types
already had a fair amount of
cess, including a win at Le Mans
lier in 1955. As a result, there was
demand from private owners both
e and in the States who wished to
them either in competition events

or purely as very exciting road cars.
An actual production line was set up
and some 42 cars were completed (not
including 9 which were either destroyed
in the factory fire or dismantled, and 16
which were made into XKSSs).

Although they were built on a production line, rather more care in construc-

1 *The Mark VIIM, recognizable externally by
its valence-mounted spot lamps, horn grilles and
indicator flashers* 2 *Probably the most exciting,
exhilarating seat of any car produced in the*

*1950s, the D-Type combined fantastic per-
formance with complete docility (J C)* 3 *The
Production D-Types allowed private owners,
particularly in the USA, to enjoy a fair degree
of success in sports car racing (J C)* 4 *The
XK140, the 120's successor, with the much
heavier bumpers and cast grille much in evidence, but otherwise with unchanged classic
shape, here in Roadster form (J C)* 5 *The
XK140 Roadster's interior was basically
unaltered, apart from detail changes such as a
better steering wheel rake, a flatter horn push
and greater leg room (J C)* 6 *This XK140
Roadster perhaps benefited from the removal of
its front bumper, often the most criticized feature of the new range (P. Porter)*

6

tion and detail work was taken, to say nothing of the testing (mainly at MIRA) prior to delivery. This was exhaustive, with one car covering as much as 650 miles on test. Of these 42 production Ds not surprisingly the largest number (some 18) were exported to the States, while the remainder were delivered as follows: Britain 10; Australia 3; France 2; and Cuba, Finland, Spain, Belgium, Mexico, New Zealand, East Africa, Canada and El Salvador received one each.

Although most of the more serious private owners received ex-works cars, nevertheless the production D-Types have between them gained over the years a tremendous number of successes up to, and including, the present. The last one to be built, in the hands of Equipe Nationale Belge, finished fourth at Le Mans in 1956 and 1957.

Apart from competition activities, the production D-Types have, over the years, provided a relatively select number of owners with sensational road performance even by today's standards, for an original price of £3,878 (I can testify to this, having been lucky enough to sample Nigel Dawes' example recently).

The XK140 introduced at the Motor Show in October 1954 was something of an enigma, because although in retrospect the car did not have the glamour of its predecessor, and the pure line was rather upset by its over-heavy bumpers, it was mechanically a superior car.

The special equipment engine of the XK120, which now produced 190 bhp, was fitted as standard, while the XK140 was also available with the C-Type head (introduced in April 1953 to the 120s) when the power rating was 210 bhp. For the first time on an XK, overdrive was offered as an optional extra, and this was found to be a very worthwhile feature, contributing to the XK140's image of a 'grand touring' car rather than a pure performance sports car. Cooling was improved with a more efficient radiator, raked to avoid the new steering rack. Contemporary road tests differed widely in their findings regarding performance, but it generally seems that, in spite of increased weight, the overall performance was slightly better than that of the XK120.

Right from the XK140's introduction all three body styles were offered. The Open or, as it has come to be known, the Roadster, differed least from its predecessor visually. Internally little was altered, although the two six-volt batteries were no longer carried behind the seats but were replaced by one twelve-

volt situated in the near-side front wing. Externally, the new models were distinguished by the larger, rather overheavy bumpers, one piece at the front and quarters at the rear. In similar vein a heavy cast grille replaced the 120's more delicate item, better headlamps and separate wing-mounted flashing indicators were incorporated, and chrome strips were added to the bonnet and boot lid, which was now several inches shorter and did not carry the number plate as previously.

It was in roadholding that the most significant changes came about. Firstly, the engine was moved three inches farther forward in the chassis. This had the effect of improving cornering by making

the car more controllable with a wei ratio of 50.3% on the front rather t the previous 47.5%. This created m leg room in the cockpit – which wa slight deficiency in the XK1 Secondly, the Burman recirculating type of steering of the former car replaced by an Alford and Alder ra and-pinion. This latest change brou complimentary comments from driv who felt that the steering was lighter more precise, and the turning circle increased from 31 ft to 33 ft. More mi changes involved the fitting of upra torsion bars and Girling telesco rather than lever-type shock absorb at the rear. UJs incorporated in the ste ing column allowed the steering wh

1

…e set at a more appropriate angle. …ome 3,354 Roadsters were produced …ll, of which only 73 were right-hand …re, and only 47 of those were intended …the British market, making this a rare …del indeed. Total price, including …chase tax of £471, was £1,598.

…ll the new XK models shared the …e mechanical specifications and …htly revised external alterations des-…ed for the Roadster. However, the …phead had another revision over …similar model of the 120, notably the …vision of two occasional rear seats. …s created what would be described …ay as a two-plus-two. These two seats …ht be adequate to carry two extra …lts down to your 'local' providing it

was very local, otherwise they were really only suitable for children, but at least it allowed the family man to enjoy XK motoring a little longer.

One can only surmise where the idea for the extra seats came from but the following may give some clues. A letter in the 28th September 1951 edition of *Autosport* from a Mr. B. W. J. Hindes of Slough read as follows: 'I thought you might be interested in the attached snap which shows my own car fitted with a third seat, which enables three fully grown adults to sit in complete comfort with the hood erected. This would surely increase the "saleability" of the vehicle (after all, we haven't all got aggressive mothers-in-law!) and I

wonder why the manufacturers do not incorporate this feature, which in my case was carried out by a local coach-building firm with very little trouble.'

Another possible inspiration may have come from the competition world. Late in 1953 Ian Appleyard had a chance of clinching the European Rally Cham-

1 *The Americans inevitably took the lion's share of XK140 Roadster production. This example is fitted with wind deflectors, although they were not a factory option (*National Motor Museum*)* **2** *Announced in 1954 concurrently with the Roadster and Fixed-Head, the XK140 Drophead Coupé was positively civilized with its folding hood and walnut dash and extra seats (*National Motor Museum*)*

pionship if he entered and was successful in the Norwegian Viking Rally. However, the regulations for this event called for four seats and therefore his 120's (RUB 120, the replacement for NUB 120 – see competition section) roadster body was replaced by a drophead body to which modifications were made to enable two small seats to be fitted behind the main ones. In fact, RUB 120 was not used on this rally because it was thought to be un-British to try and beat the rules, but it may have

been the inspiration for the 140 dropheads, of which 479 rhd and 2,310 lhd cars were built at just £46 more than the open two-seater.

The 140 DHC was the all-rounder XK, open but with a civilized hood with larger rear window than the 120, reasonable interior space, more or less the classic line and mechanically superior to the 120s.

Of the trio, the fixed-head was the most altered. Sharing all the modifications of the Roadster and the drophead,

excluding the adoption of a single ▐ tery but including the occasional ▐ seats, the FHC went a stage further addition to the extra 3 inches gai▐ from moving the engine forward, ▐ bulkhead was modified to surround ▐ engine, thus giving greater leg room ▐ allowing the seats to be moved forw▐ some 12 inches. This, plus extending ▐ back of the roof by a further 6½ inc▐ combined with the moving forwar▐ the windscreen a fraction, provided s▐ stantially more room. A larger ▐

1

2

dow and larger rear quarter-lights
tributed to this effect.

he fixed-heads were fitted with
nger-type door handles as opposed to
then more common lever type, as can
be seen on the dropheads. All the
s at 14 ft 8 in were 3 inches longer
their predecessors because of the
bumpers.

ist price for the Fixed Heads was
16 for the basic model, and a further
4 for the Special Equipment 210 bhp
del. Some 2,808 fixed-heads were

produced in all, made up of 843 rhd and
1,965 lhd models. In the States, as
before, the Special Equipment models
were known as 140Ms, the M standing

for 'modified'. When fitted with the C-
Type head they were designated
XK140MCs.

*1 In the XK140 Drophead Coupé only minimal
space was allocated to the so-called extra seats
(JC)* **2** *The 140 DHC had a pleasing shape
even with the hood raised, but although fitted
with a larger rear window than its predecessor,
rear threequarter vision was restricted (JC)* **3**

*Clearly visible is the extra length of the 'fixed-
head' portion of the XK140 FHC (JC)* **4**
*Looking happier with wire wheels, the 140 did
not shirk an occasional competitive event*
(National Motor Museum)

6 THE XK EVOLVES

Whilst the Jaguar sports cars brought the 'Pace', and the large saloons the 'Grace and Space', the company needed a production car to boost turnover and the new compact range filled that niche in the company's armoury. The later fifties saw gradual improvement in all models rather than dramatic developments – but these were at the planning stage.

ree years of design and development
[wor]k and one million pounds' worth of
[too]ling yielded the new 2.4-litre small
[salo]on in 1955. This was a most import-
[ant] model which, with refinements and
[a va]riety of engine sizes, was to be in pro-
[duc]tion until 1969. It started to appear
[on] the roads in 1956 – a remarkable year
[for] Jaguar and Sir William Lyons,
[bec]ause he was knighted in the New
[Yea]r's Honours' List. In the same year
[tha]t Jaguar won at Le Mans and Reims,
[the]y won the famous Monte Carlo Rally,
[ma]king the company the first ever to win

both Le Mans and the 'Monte', and a
further compliment was accorded the
company with an official visit by Queen
Elizabeth II and the Duke of Edinburgh.
The remarkable XK engine continued to
power these winning cars, the compact
range, the large saloon and, from 1957,
the ultimate development of the XK
range – the XK150s.

But all was not rosy during this period
because on 12th February 1957 fire
broke out in the factory and spread
rapidly. It was brought under control
before it reached catastrophic propor-

tions but enough damage had been done
to upset production considerably. The
damage was thought to total £3½ million,
but with ingenuity and co-operation the
factory and production recovered

1, 2 *In 1956 Sir William Lyons and Jaguar
were accorded the honour of a Royal visit, as
Her Majesty inspects the Le Mans winning D-
Type with her host and visits the shop floor
(J C)* **3** *The announcement of the new 'com-
pact' 2.4-litre sporting saloon, which was to
prove of enormous importance to Jaguar sales
(J C)*

remarkably quickly, and 1957 turned out to be a record year for output.

For the Tourist Trophy Meeting at Dundrod in 1954 Jaguar had produced a new 2½-litre version of the XK engine for two of the D-Types in an attempt to beat the handicappers, who were notoriously hard on the larger-engined cars. This engine reappeared in the completely new small saloon at the 1955 Earls Court Show.

Most important in 1955 was that this was the first production Jaguar to be built of unitary construction instead of traditional chassis and unstressed body construction of all the previous models. The D-Type had pioneered this type of construction for Jaguar, although in a rather different form, and it was certainly progress in the right direction.

The suspension was also different, being a coil spring and wishbone arrangement carried on a separate rubber-mounted subframe at the front and a rear suspension of trailing arms with cantilever semi-elliptic springs. New Lockheed Brakemaster-type hydraulic brakes were fitted all round, aided by servo assistance. Although this was something of an economy Jaguar, all the usual refinements such as wa[l] dash, controls and door cappi[n] leather upholstery and so on w[ere] included in the specification of the [2.4] which weighed some 27 cwt. Includ[ing] purchase tax, the 2.4 retailed at £1,[ ] for the special equipment model, wh[ich] included a heater, central armr[est] Jaguar mascot, vitreous enamel[led] manifolds and an electric clock. With [the] optional Laycock de Normanville ov[er] drive, the new model was just capabl[e of] the magic 100 mph, and would re[ach] 60 mph from standstill in just [ ] seconds. Viewed now, the car looks v[ery]

1

ed, with its heavy pillars and full rear wheel spats, but at the time it was well received.

Towards the end of 1956, the Mark VIII appeared. Essentially similar to its predecessors, it had however a few important changes. It was fitted with a B-Type-headed engine, which produced ... bhp in this form with twin SU HD6 carburettors. The B-Type without reference to the alphabet had been developed from the C-Type head. It differed in that it had an inlet valve angle ... 5°. This resulted in a useful improvement at the lower and middle rev ranges

and slightly better overall performance. The extra power was somewhat offset by extra weight created by extra refinements – not that the three cigar lighters now fitted would have altered things appreciably, but it all added up.

Visually the Mark VIII differed from the Mark VII in four noticeable ways. First and foremost the dated V-type split windscreen was replaced by a curved one-piece item. The radiator grille was re-styled and a chrome strip followed the wing line down the sides, breaking up the slab effect. Finally the rear wheel spats were slightly cut away, again

relieving those large slab sides. To further lighten the body style and follow fashion, the Mark VIIIs were generally finished in two-tone paint. More subtly,

1 *A one-piece windscreen, chrome surround to the radiator grille and side chrome body moulding immediately distinguish the Mark VIII* (National Motor Museum) **2** *More at home in its native country, where it was listed at £1,299, the 2.4 was very popular* (J C) **3** *A couple of 2.4 saloons involved in high-speed testing at the banked MIRA track, where they proved themselves capable of 100 mph in spite of their smaller engine* (N. Dewis)

2

3

a chromium-plated radiator surround and leaping Jaguar mascot adorned the front end.

This, then, was the Mark VIII climbing, as we would say today, up market, in an attempt to steal more and more customers from those two fine cars – Bentley and Rolls-Royce.

Late in 1956 the XKSS was created and became available at the beginning of the following year. It is said that due to lack of demand, amazingly enough, for production D-Types (substantiated in an advertisement in an *Autosport* of 1958 for a 'brand new D-Type nearly £1,000 under list price' – that is, £2,995!) several semi-completed cars were sitting around 'going rusty' when Sir William had the idea of clearing them by turning them into more civilized road cars. This is just one of several theories about the birth of the XKSS. Another was that it was to enable owners to compete in production car racing in the States; whereas Duncan Hamilton also claims the credit for the idea, having converted his first D, OKV 1, into a more refined car for its subsequent owner, the late 'Jumbo' Goddard.

The XKSS differed from an ordinary production D in various details. The centre division between driver and passenger was removed and a full width screen was provided. The headrest fairing was not fitted, but a door for the passenger was. The car sprouted front and rear quarter bumpers and a baggage rack mounted on the rear. Some extra trimming to the interior and rudimentary sidescreens and hood added a little to creature comforts.

Sadly, production was halted abruptly by the fire when only 16 XKSSs had been completed. Of these, 12 went to the States, two to Canada, one to Hong Kong and one remained in Britain. Two D-Types were converted by the factory to XKSSs, making a total of 18 all told.

In the aftermath of the near disastrous fire, the company launched a natural progression of the small car range – the 2.4 saloon but with the more usual 3442 cc version of the XK engine. This unit, with twin SU HD6 carburettors, high lift cams and a dual exhaust system, produced 210 bhp at 5,000 rpm and gave the 3.4, as it was known, a very useful performance. A genuine top speed of 120 mph, acceleration from standing start to 60 mph in 11.7 seconds and the standing quarter-mile in 17.9 seconds ensured that this was no sluggard and, as usual, kept Jaguar in front of its competitors.

Mechanical changes were made to take the extra weight and power of the larger engine. The engine mountings were modified, the suspension stiffened, and besides the larger grille and badges the main distinguishing feature between the two models was that the new addition had cut-away rear wheel spats. Manual, manual with overdrive, and Borg Warner automatic transmission were the options, and the last of these, although slower, still gave a brisk performan with 60 mph reached in 11.2 seconds

From September 1957 the 3.4's w grille was adopted on the smaller v sion. Disc brakes could be ordered both models from the beginning of 19 and automatic transmission was i available on the smaller car as well.

An area in which both the XK120

140 had very definitely not been up
tandard was in braking. Fade had
ys been a problem and the few small
ifications over the years had made
e real improvement. Some new
elopment was obviously needed, and
racing indisputedly improved the
d. The XK150 appeared in May
7, fitted with Dunlop disc brakes,
which had first been used by Jaguar on
the C-Type in the 1952 Mille Miglia.
Disc brakes were a subject of considerable collaboration and development

*1 The rear spats of the Mark VIII had also
come in for attention and contributed to the
updating of the flagship (J C) 2 Members of
Royalty were tempted to try the XKSS, the*

*thinly disguised D-Type, here being sampled by
Prince Michael of Kent with Norman Dewis
(N. Dewis) 3 The XKSS was never a very
photogenic car but looked much happier in the
flesh (J C) 4 Prince Philip was not always content (as shown here) to be a passenger in an
XKSS, and insisted on taking the controls
when out of sight of his entourage 5 A curved
windscreen, fixed side windows, two doors and
a hood made the XKSS almost civilized (J C)*

5

The fitting of the 3.4-litre engine to the smaller saloons gave them typical Jaguar performance (J C)

between Dunlop and Jaguar, and they played a great part in Jaguar's success on the track, particularly in long-distance racing, in which the Ferraris experienced brake fade with their then conventional drum brakes. These new Dunlop brakes were quoted as being 'the greatest single weapon which demolished the opposition' in the 1953 Vingt-Quatre Heures du Mans, when the three works C-Types finished in first, second and fourth places.

So, four years later, Jaguar introduced similar disc brakes on a production car in the shape of the XK150. Only fixed-head and drophead models were announced initially. The factory could not at this juncture cope with heavy re-tooling with other work on hand, so by cleverly compromising, they were able to use much of the 120/140 tooling. The exterior design of the car, although still very much an XK, was nevertheless significantly different from the XK120 and 140. The wing line, which had fallen and risen so dramatically on the earlier cars, in contrast was almost straight. The bonnet was wider with the addition of a fillet down the centre to reduce new tooling, making access to the engine a good deal easier. The windscreen was of one-piece design and the walnut dashboard was gone, replaced initially by aluminium and later by leather. The XK150 was a step further away from the out-and-out, wind-in-your-hair type of sports car introduced in 1948 and a step nearer to the ultra comfortable, ultra sophisticated grand touring car announced in 1961. This is not to decry the car, but is merely a reflection of the times and Jaguar's business policy.

The fixed-head illustrated here would have cost you £1,763 in the UK at the time of its announcement, just £123 more than the Special Equipment XK120 of 1953. So much for inflation. . . .

The interiors on both models benefited from the thinner doors, with shoulder room being increased by four inches, which made the car a lot more comfortable. Like the 140, the 150 had the two small occasional rear seats, but the heating layout, also similar to the

1, 2 Such was the gravity of Jaguar's fire in postwar Britain that the disaster did not go unnoticed – even in the very highest circles (J C) 3 The sad remains of an XKSS and a damaged D-Type were among the casualties of the terrible fire of 1957 (J C) 4 The Duke of Kent collects his new 3.4 from Lofty England, showing Royalty's preference for Jaguars (National Motor Museum)

74

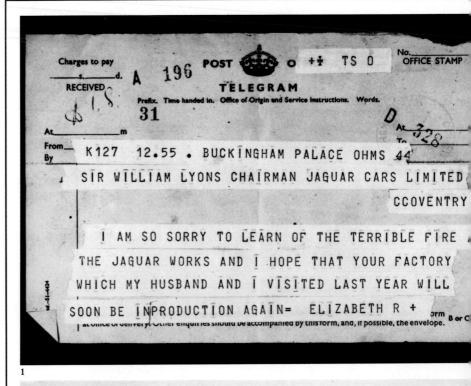

1

10 Downing Street
Whitehall

February 13, 1957

Dear Sir William Lyons

I am indeed sorry to hear of the disaster which has struck your firm. Jaguar cars have been doing a magnificent job in our battle for exports and it is tragic luck that you have received this blow. But I am confident that with your customary energy and courage you will get production going in a very short time. I am the more encouraged in this belief by the accounts of the wonderful work done by your workers in helping to save the most important part of your factory.

I am sincerely
Harold Macmillan

2

URW 510

140, was now primitive in comparison with its competitors. In several respects, including the poor front seats (they were virtually a bench with their lack of support, which inhibited enthusiastic cornering), the XK150 was starting to show its age, in comparison with say, the 300 SL Mercedes Benz, the BMW 507 and the DB2/4 Aston Martin. But in fairness it must be stated that the basic XK design dated back to 1948 and its rivals were much more expensive. The basic XK150 DHC when introduced was, as stated, £1,783 (including purchase tax), whereas the 300 SL cost £4,651, the

BMW £4,201 and the DB2/4 £2,889. Not surprisingly, the XK150 was the heaviest XK, at some 29½ cwt.

Initially two power options were available. The standard car fitted with the 140 engine gave 190 bhp. However, a special equipment model was also available and this was usually fitted with a 210 bhp engine. This latter unit was fitted with the B-Type head. This produced more torque rather than any great increase in power.

The XK150 was the first sports car to have the leaping Jaguar mascot to be officially offered as an optional extra.

At that time, American cars w sporting pretensions were being fi with larger and larger V8 engines a although they could not live with an when it came to cornering or stopp some were faster in a straight l Jaguar, conscious of this, and also of performance of the various Ita exotica, made efforts to improve the

To those visiting the Earls Co Motor Show in 1958, the new Mark which succeeded the Mark VIII, seer little different, but under the skin sev important changes had been made to yet more sophistication to Jaguar's f

Not surprisingly, disc brakes were fitted all round as standard and, [bet]ter late than never, the large saloon [was] at last fitted with power assisted [stee]ring, a facility the Americans had [been] used to for many years on their own [cars] and a department in which they had [criti]cized the Jaguars. The assistance [was] provided by a Hobourn-Eaton [pum]p driven off the rear end of the [gen]erator, and a useful side effect was [that] this allowed the steering to be [gear]ed up to require only three-and-a-[half] turns from lock to lock, which suited [thos]e with sporting pretensions.

The Mark IX had an enlarged version of the faithful XK engine. Capacity was increased to 3.8 litres (3781 cc). It was the first time a production Jaguar had been fitted with this unit, although a number of examples had been on active service on the race tracks of the world in 1957 and 1958, particularly in the successful Lister sports racing cars.

This new engine improved the Mark IX's performance over that of the Mark VIII by a useful margin. Acceleration from 0 to 60 took just 11 seconds, and top speed was now more than 110 mph. Naturally, this had to be paid

1 'Partners in Power' was the title of Dunlop's advertising campaign, featuring the disc brake and the XK150 (Dunlop) 2 One of the legends of motoring journalism, John Bolster, about to try the new XK150 Fixed Head (National Motor Museum) 3 Now more of a grand touring car, the XK150, in Drophead guise, was a further step away from the out-and-out sports car introduced in 1948 (J C) 4 The line of the XK150 DHC was pleasant enough but in practice the folded hood made rearward vision far from satisfactory (J C) 5 The S insignia below the front quarterlight identifies the triple carb, straight port-headed version of the XK150 (J C)

for, which meant £2,163 for the automatic version and a consumption of around 14 miles per gallon. This was not surprising when you consider that the car weighed 35 cwt.

A 1958 Jaguar sales brochure stated: 'For many the choice of a sports car means only one thing – a roadster; for this is the type of model from which all other sports cars have been derived and which alone possesses the classical sports car "line"'. And so, at the beginning of 1958, a Roadster XK150 was announced and with it came the optional S version.

The S had a further refined cylinder head, which had been developed by Harry Weslake. Known as the 'straight port head', because of the partial straightening of the ports, thereby increasing the flow of mixture at high revolutions, it was also fed by no less than three 2-inch SU carburettors. The engine was also fitted with a stronger clutch, lightened flywheel and lead-bronze bearings.

The result of this was that the car could reach 60 mph in 7.3 seconds and had a top speed of 133 mph. The Americans were quick to note that here was a car that was 'designed' to travel at these speeds, and consequently felt safer and more controllable.

In other respects the Roadster was similar to its predecessors, but with the 150 modifications. It was still a pure two-seater but less stark, which caused raised eyebrows amongst some diehards when they noted that it had wind-up windows.

Later, the S engine was offered on the fixed-head and drophead coupés as well. Searching for still more performance, Jaguar announced in 1960 that the 3.8-litre XK engine, which had already been offered in the Mark IX, was to be available in the XK150. The 3.8 could be had either with the B-Type head, or with the straight port head, whence it became known as the 3.8S. The latter was the ultimate production XK, with a power output of 265 bhp, giving a top speed of 136 mph. In acceleration, the car was actually slightly slower at lower speeds than the 3.4, but gained considerably nearer its maximum. The problem now, with its live rear axle, was to get the power down on the road efficiently.

Towards the end of 1959 Jaguar updated and improved the small saloon range and added a 3.8 model. Because these were called MK 2s, their predecessors have logically come to be known as MK 1s, although they were never officially so-called.

The appearance of the cars was considerably improved, as was vision, by a much larger wrap-around rear window and more slender pillars all round, accentuated by the use of chrome window frames. The facelift included a new grille with a central rib, faired-in sidelights on top of the wings, and horn grilles replaced by spotlights. The interior was also altered and equipped with a new and much superior instrument layout.

An increased rear track (by 3¾ inches) contributed to greater stability at speed, which had been a problem on ea[r] models; and the front suspension given a higher roll centre. Disc br[a] were no longer optional – they w standard, and drivers found repeated use at high speeds caused loss of stopping power or uneven[n] nor did it require an increase in p[e] pressure. A brake fluid level warr light was added to the specification.

Three models of Mark 2s were av able. These were the 2.4, with

1

2

roved B-Type head producing
bhp at 5750 rpm; the 3.4, which
inued to give 210 bhp; and the 3.8,
seen in the Mark IX a year earlier.
last-named engine had a 87 mm
e compared with the 83 mm of the
unit. In producing 220 bhp it lost
ing of its smoothness or flexibility,
made useful gains in torque –
b ft at 3000 rpm compared to the
215 lb ft.
his largest-engined version, which

also had a limited slip differential fitted,
was an excellent high performance
saloon with few if any rivals – certainly
not at £1,842 15s 10d for the manual
with overdrive. Its vivid acceleration in
third gear on wet roads could easily
cause wheelspin. And in competition
3.8s clocked up a prodigious number of
wins in subsequent years.

A contemporary motoring magazine
came to the conclusion that the 3.4
offered an 'outstanding combination of

1, 2 More for export than for home consumption, the XK150 Roadster, as it has come to be known, was officially called the Open. Unlike the Drophead, it had an uninterrupted rear view (National Motor Museum) 3 Like the XK150, the Mark IX was the final version of a theme started at the beginning of the decade (J C) 4 The disc brakes fitted to the Mark IX were now even more necessary with the 3.8 engine (J C)

speed, refinement and true driving ease.' The Mark 2 models were to be of immense business importance to the company because while the competition models provided the image and publicity, the sports models the excitement, and the executive range the prestige, the compact saloons contributed most to the turnover, stability and steadily increasing profits of the company. Nearly 100,000 Mark 2s were produced. It should be remembered that while many firms have had periods of difficulty and a great many famous names have disappeared for good, Jaguar have sailed happily on with full order books at all times, or at least until the late 1970s.

The order placed by the Nottingham police for a number of Brough Superiors fitted with Swallow sidecars set a precedent that was to continue to the present day. Postwar Mark V saloons were favoured by several forces, but it was the later Mark 1 and 2 saloons that proved particularly popular, especially for patrolling the newly opened M1, which at that time had no speed limit at all. These saloons provided the police with just what they required: reliability and performance at a sensible price.

The XK engines were put to good use in vehicles other than cars. They were used in Dennis fire tenders and in various military vehicles, and required

little modification. When fitted to Alvis Scorpion and Scimitar armou vehicles a military-type distributor fitted, the heads were altered in exhaust valve region to meet the requ ments of heavily leaded fuel, and a s carburettor replaced the normal SUs

It is no coincidence that many of original Jaguar distributors and age prospered and continue to pros

1 *The Kent family remained loyal to marque, Prince Michael being among the first to aquire a new Mark 2 saloon (J C)* 2 *chrome side window frames of the Mark 2 much to modernize and lighten the sm saloon range (J C)*

JAGUAR IN COLOUR

Colour is, and always has been, important to Jaguar, being a vital ingredient of style and individuality – both important features in the Jaguar story. The Swallows and SSs were boldly coloured, distinguishing them in an otherwise dour era. The post-war colour range was extensive and incorporated a selection of highly effective 'opalescent' finishes. Today, new colours are helping to popularize the current range.

R.M.V. 'Soapy' Sutton about to achieve 132 mph in a standard XK120 Roadster with the normal screens removed (J C)

1

2

3

2 *The central slat to the radiator dis-
guishes the Mark II Austin Seven Swallow
oon, fitted here with ships' ventilators atop
scuttle and clearly showing the 'peak'* **3** *The
I Tourer offered SS style with open motor-
and four seats (J C)* **4** *The delightful rakish
es of the SS 100, together with its lively per-
mance combine to make the model one of the
st revered of all sports cars (J C)* **5** *From
to right: a 1½ sv Saloon, an SS 100 and
SS 1 Saloon (J C)*

4

1

2

3

4

6

high proportion of SS100s survive today
wing their owners to still appreciate their
e and respectable turn of speed **2** Jaguar's
 new postwar model, the Mark V, clearly
ws the prewar influence but was to be the
l manifestation of that line (JC) **3** The
 threequarter vision must have been appal-
on the Mark V Drophead Coupé, but there
o denying the car had style (JC) **4** Leslie
nson's XK120 before the start of the 1949
duction Car Race at Silverstone, the car's
ng début and first of countless victories **5**
ther view of Johnson's car which was in fact
 second left-hand drive XK120 built and
 converted to right-hand drive (JC) **6**
at XKs were popular for club racing can
rly be seen from this Le Mans-type start
C)

5

1 *The first C-Type, XKC 001, photographed at the factory before being shipped over to Dundrod where Johnson and Rolt finished third behind team mates Moss and Walker in the 1951 TT (J C)* 2 *Here Moss pilots C-Type XKC 053, which he shared at Le Mans in 1953 with Peter Walker, to second place behind the similar car of Rolt and Hamilton (J C)* 3 *Norman Dewis is congratulated by Lofty England after recording the amazing speed of 172 mph at Jabbeke in Belgium (J C)* 4, 5 *This D-Type, XKC 404, was one of the original trio of works Ds for 1954, the model's first victory being the 12-hour event at Rheims. OKV 3 continues to be actively and successfully campaigned today in international historic racing by Martin Morris (J C)*

1

1

1 *This Mark VII Saloon belonged to H.M. The Queen Mother for a number of years and was partially updated to Mark VIII specification, which explains the one-piece windscreen (J C)* **2** *An XK150 Roadster with an interesting selection of optional extras displayed behind (J C)* **3** *The XK150 'S' Roadster in 3.8-litre right-hand-drive form was produced in very limited quantities (J C)* **4** *Jaguar's Mark 2 Saloon was an obvious choice for the police to use for patrolling Britain's first motorway, the M1 (J C)* **5** *The Mark 2 Saloons were immensely popular and remained in production from 1959 to 1967 (J C)*

1 *A very early pre-production E-Type on test at MIRA. Note the absence of chrome rims to the headlamp glasses* (JC) 2 *Even today, over 30 years on, the Series One E-Type remains a sensationally exciting shape* (JC) 3 *This E-Type underbonnet view shows the designers' success in carrying out Lyons' original dictum – that the engine was to be a glamorous one* (JC) 4 *A Series One Fixed Head E-Type, displaying its pure, clean lines* (JC) 5 *Sir William Lyons' dollar-earning flagship for the 1960s, the Mark X, in front of his magnificent home, Wappenbury Hall* (JC)

I

2

4

1 *The independent rear suspension unit developed for the E-Type and Mark X, and subsequently used on the interim S-Type and 420, and more latterly the XJ range (J C)* **2** *An early example of an XJ6, the range that was to carry Jaguar's fortunes through the 1970s and early 1980s (J C)* **3** *The Series Three E-Type introduced the brilliant V12 engine to the world (J C)* **4** *The closed V12E was offered only as a '2 + 2' and like its open sister was introduced in 1971 (J C)* **5** *The XJ, seen here in Series Two form, continued the long partnership between the police forces of Great Britain and the Jaguar company (J C)*

1

1 *The sensational XJ13: exciting because of its styling, an extension of the C/D, D, E theme, its mid-engine configuration, and four-overhead cam V12, but sad because it was never seen in action* (J C) 2, 3, 4, 5 *Interesting styling exercises, about which little is known, but perhaps a replacement for the E-Type was being contemplated* (J C) 6 *The XJS undergoing wind-tunnel tests* (J C) 7 *Often described as a 'plumber's nightmare', the underbonnet area of the XJS with the V12 engine installed left little room to spare* (J C) 8 *The XJS, whilst not a sports car, was a 'grand touring' car in the sense of the phrase's original definition – a car capable of carrying its occupants at high speed and in great comfort* (J C)

1

2

3

4

5

1 *The Group 44 XJ27 with the V12 engine installed amidships was surely designed and built with Le Mans ultimately in mind and was entered for the '84 race (J C)* **2** *The two most important men in Jaguar history. On the right, Sir William Lyons, founder, former Chairman and Life President, with Chief Executive, John Egan (J C)* **3** *A typical Jaguar motor show stand of the early 1950s showing a Mark VII Saloo surrounded by an XK120 Roadster, Fixed Hea and two Dropheads (J C)*

The TWR built and prepared XJSs dominated the 1984 European Touring Car Championship and helped to forge a most significant partnership. (Jaguar Cars)

That partnership was taken a stage further when TWR were entrusted with Jaguar's return to the field of international sports car racing for which they built the XJR–6. (Jaguar Cars)

For 1987 the traditional green livery was
dropped in favour of the colours of major
sponsors, Silk Cut. (Philip Porter)

The partnership really paid off in 1988 with victory at Le
Mans, a result that guarantees worldwide publicity, as Jaguar
...overed in the fifties. (Jaguar Cars)

Below A striking livery was created for the IMSA cars raced by
TWR in the States in 1988 and which began and concluded the
season with victories. (Jaguar Cars)

Previous pages: The XJS V12 Convertible at last brought rather more style to this model which had enjoyed a chequered career until the mid-eighties. (Jaguar Cars)

The entire future of the Jaguar company rested on the acceptability or otherwise of the new XJ40 replacement for the final Lyons masterpiece, the XJ6. (Philip Porter)

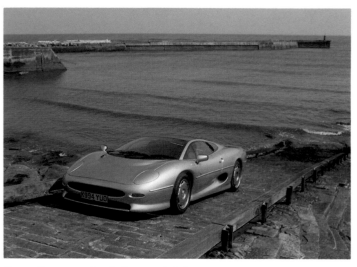

...anks to the radical, all-conquering XJR-14, which was closely based on ...rent Formula One practise, Jaguar clinched the 1991 World Sportscar ...ampionship, their third in five years. (Jaguar Cars)

JaguarSport translated the superb XJ220 concept by Jim Randle and colleagues, and a brilliant piece of automotive styling by Keith Helfet, into a breathtaking masterpiece. (Philip Porter)

...ensational example of automotive sculpture though the XJ220 was, it was also a tremendous tribute to the engineers for the car was a quantum leap in ...formance terms, yet relatively practical and uniquely refined for such a car. (Philip Porter)

The latest saloon range, which was unveiled in late 1994 a[nd] might unofficially be termed the Series V XJ6, was the first [new] model to be substantially influenced by the Ford takeover. T[his] is the ultra sporty XJR model (Jaguar Cars)

The performance of the exciting XJR supercharged mo[del] gave the six-cylinder version comparable acceleration to [the] XJ12 saloon without the fuel consumption penalties. T[his] model proved so popular that V12 sales suffered (Jag[uar] Cars)

ough a few have been lost to the
que, thanks to British Leyland's
chise policy.

rom the start, Brown and Mallalieu,
whom Lyons had worked briefly, and
kers, were agents for Blackpool and
nchester respectively. When Lyons
ted Birmingham, he met up with the
ners of P. J. Evans, later known for
hile as Broad Street Motors. They
e appointed distributors for the Mid-
ds. Henlys became distributors for
south, and over the years have
eloped into a very large group.
he later distributors and dealers list
ds like a Who's Who of famous
ges. It included H. R. Owen, Mann

Eggerton, Blue Star Garages, Lex
Garages, Rowland Smith, Rossleigh,
Martin Walter, Charles Follett, Sydney
Marcus, Harold Radford and Kennings,
to name but a few. Others, not surpris-
ingly, were involved in Jaguar competi-
tion history. These included Sammy
Newsome, John Coombs, HW Motors,
Ian Appleyard, Dickie Attwood, Archie
Scott Brown, Reg Mansbridge, Robin
Sturgess, the Stewarts (Jimmy and
Jackie), Dick Protheroe and many oth-
ers who, like the above, were either the
owners or the sons of owners. Many,
such as Rothwell and Milbourne of
Malvern and Ritchies of Glasgow, were
loyal to the make for many years.

1 It is hard to believe that the Mark 2 could carry all this equipment and still be ideal for high-speed pursuits (J C) 2 The mobile theme taken up by Jaguar's largest distributor, although in a rather more sophisticated form (National Motor Museum)

7 THE E ARRIVES

Sensation returned to the Jaguar image with the unleashing of the dramatic E-Type sports car and later the prestigious Mark X. Export took on an even greater significance for the company and its products demanded and received renewed respect. The smaller saloons continued with refinements and added variations and brought practical Jaguar motoring to a wider audience.

1

2

3

re was no denying that in 1961 the 150, good car though it was, was coming a little dated in comparison some of the competition, and ainly by Jaguar standards. Sir Wil- and his team had been working on eplacement since 1957. They had ned a lot from the racing D-Types in March, a new Jaguar, the sensa- al E-Type, was unleashed on the ld. The world was stunned, dards changed overnight, com- tors reeled, and Jaguars were back at forefront of sports car design.

ater that year the factory introduced a completely new, and at the time very dramatic, large saloon car, the Mark X. Both these models received considerable acclaim across the Atlantic, earning very many dollars for Britain, and both reflected the increasing technical merit of Jaguar products.

The E-Type, arguably the most famous sports car of all time, has certainly become a household name and a synonym for speed. Introduced at the Geneva Motor Show in March 1961, there were two versions available – the open two-seater Roadster and the two-seater Fixed Head Coupé.

Closely derived from the D-Type of Le Mans fame, and again a perfect example of racing improving the breed, the E

1 *Sir William Lyons poses with his ultimate sports car at Geneva in March 1961* (Autocar) 2 *E1A, the first step down the road to the legendary E-Type* (N. Dewis) 3, 5, 6 *Rather nearer to its final form, this car seen on test from a variety of angles is presumed to be the one affectionately known in the factory as 'the pop rivet special'* (N. Dewis) 4 *The famous road-test Fixed Head, 9600 HP, that set the 150 mph legend when tested by most of the major motoring journals* (Autocar)

6

shared a similar monocoque centre section to which was attached sub-frames front and rear to carry the front suspension, steering and engine, and the rear independent suspension and differential, respectively. Fitted with the XK engine in 3.8 form, triple carburettors and four-speed box, allied to the overall lightness of the car, it boasted a staggering performance for its day.

The biggest deviation from the D-Type theme was in the rear suspension. Independent suspension had been tried on a D, and was further developed on E2A, the second prototype, which was raced for a while by Briggs Cunningham (including Le Mans in 1960), but this was the first time it had been used on a production Jaguar. Certainly it contributed greatly to the car's high standard of ride, roadholding and overall performance. The car's braking, only just about adequate for the performance, featured disc brakes all round, inboard at the rear. The only department in which the 3.8s could be, and have been, seriously criticized was the gearbox. It was heavy and very slow, and slightly marred the overall pleasure of the performance.

The E-Type, unlike the XK150, w[as] not available with either overdrive [or] automatic transmission – there w[as] simply no room.

The original Jaguar brochure open[ed] with the sentence, 'No more fam[ous] background can be found anywhere th[an] that which lies behind the Jaguar [E-] Type GT (Grand Touring) Models'. [It] then went on to name the models as 't[he] Jaguar E-Type GT Fixed-Head Cou[pé] and the Jaguar E-Type GT Open Tw[o-] Seater'. Interestingly, like the origi[nal] XK120, correctly entitled the Op[en] Two-Seater Super Sports, but whi[ch]

1
2
3
4

come to be known simply as the
...dster, somewhere along the line the
... was also dropped from the E-Type's
... The same brochure concluded its
...mble with the modest claim that 'the
...ar E-Type GT is, in truth, the most
...anced sports car in the world'. Few,
...ny, would have disagreed with this
...ment.

...or 1962 a few minor revisions were
...le. Notably the bonnet, which had
...n opened by a T handle inserted into
...hes on the exterior, was now released
...nternal catches. The bonnet louvres,
...ch on early cars had been a separate

panel let into the centre section, became
a one-piece integral pressing. And a little
more leg room was achieved by means
of a 'dish' in the floor. A slight inden-
tation in the rear bulkhead allowed the
seats to be moved slightly further back
for taller occupants.

Prices stood at £1,830 for the Roadster and £1,954 for the fixed-head. Production figures for the 3.8s were 7,827
and 7,669 for the Roadster and Fixed-
head, respectively.

The E-Type's performance is well
known. It had a top speed of around
150 mph, and a 0–60 mph time of 6.9

seconds, with consumption in the area of
16–20 mpg, depending on whether you
were pressing or pottering.

What is not quite so well known is that
the original fixed-head road-test car
(registered 9600 HP and now owned by

*1 The press were riveted by the sports car's
dramatic appeal (Autocar) 2 In this seat you
could travel at 150 mph – still a legal speed in
1961 (Autocar) 3 Lyons's original dictum was
fulfilled: the engine was indeed a glamorous
piece of machinery (Autocar) 4 Sir William
Lyons enters 77 RW, the original open-road
test car at a Jaguar Silver Jubilee gathering
(National Motor Museum)*

the author), had one or two novel features. 'The car that created the 150 mph legend' as it has been described, had an aluminium rear tailgate in place of the normal steel, perspex windows, and an interesting engine.

The E-Type in standard form would not, in fact, do a genuine 150 mph, and later models have always appeared slower by comparison with those original figures. But this is mere quibbling today when we have blanket speed limits and dense traffic, to say nothing of most of the drivers. The E-Type was and is a very fast car.

Following closely on the announcement of the E-Type came the new 'top of the range' big saloon, the Mark X. Replacing the Mark IX, the new car was a considerable step forward rather than a mere updating of a concept. Gone was the chassis, the construction being of a monocoque type in line with other models. The styling, while bearing some family resemblance, was generally rather different. Designed with the US market in mind, it was extremely large, and wider than any other British car of the

period. The reverse slant to the f end, incorporating the fashionable headlamps, was distinctive.

The Mark X shared a good deal the sports car. Most notable was the f independent rear suspension, wl gave the car a high standard of ride cornering. This incorporated on side a lower transverse tubular pivoted at the wheel carrier and the frame adjacent to the differential ca and, above this, a half shaft univers jointed at each end. These serve locate the wheel in a transverse pl

1

2

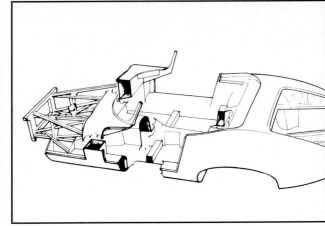

3

gitudinal location was provided by
er mountings, which located the
assembly to the body structure and
adius arms between the lower links
the mounting points on the body.
n-coil springs, each enclosing a tele-
ic hydraulic damper, provided the
ension medium.

he front suspension was also an
pendent arrangement and in-
orated double wishbones and coil
gs with telescopic shock absorbers.
nti-roll bar was located between the
r wishbones. The complete assem-

bly, together with steering gear, was
mounted on a separate sub-frame, which
was itself located in the body by rubber
mountings.

To power this very big car (the boot
alone had a capacity of 27 cu ft) which
weighed 35 cwt, Jaguar provided the 3.8
engine with three SU carburettors, first

1 Few Es found their way on to the home market in 1961, but this car, now registered XVE 1, the first of the line, went to Henlys as their demonstration model 2 For the first time, an open Two-Seater Jaguar could be had with a hard top – the external bonnet release lock of the very early cars is visible (J C) 3 The monocoque and sub-frame construction of the E-Type (J C) 4

There was a strong family resemblance between the E-Type and its racing forbear, the D 5 The dramatic new flagship, the Mark X, enabled Lyons to 'steal' another Motor Show 6 The counter-balanced forward-hinging bonnet of the Mark X was an innovation for a Jaguar saloon, as were the 14-in diameter wheels (National Motor Museum)

6

The original E-Type had a clean, aerodynamic shape (J C)

seen in the XK150S and used subsequently in the E-Type. With an output of 265 bhp at 5,500 rpm, it gave the Mark X a lively, if not staggering performance and an average fuel consumption of 16–18 mpg, although fast motoring could reduce this to 12 mpg. Fuel for this thirsty animal was carried in two 10-gallon tanks in the rear wings.

Most cars were fitted with automatic transmission, but manual transmission could still be specified, with or without overdrive. In practice, few manual versions were produced. Comfort was of a high order, with leather seats, and very full instrumentation laid out in the usual Jaguar tradition, surrounded by walnut. Electrically operated windows became an optional extra for the first time on a Jaguar.

Needless to say, the car was a great success. It caused a sensation at the Earls Court Motor Show, and earned yet more dollars for Britain. As usual, journalists vied with each other to think of more and greater superlatives. Denis Holmes, writing in the *Daily Mail*, after claiming 'It's new; it's astounding; it's unequalled', reached his verdict with 'The chauffeur will have to beg to be allowed to drive'.

With regard to the dollars earned, Jaguar were able to announce, 'At the end of an all-day meeting between Jaguar and their American and Canadian distributors, orders were placed to a total of 63 million dollars ($£22\frac{1}{2}$ million). This represents a doubling of the demand for Jaguar in the North American continent, and results from the widening of the scope of the Jaguar range following the introduction of the new Mark X saloon. This order will stretch the production capacity of the factory to its utmost even allowing for the expansion programme already in hand. A strict delivery schedule has been written into the contract and orders not executed on time will be automatically cancelled. Sir William said at Earls Court recently "This order represents the biggest challenge in our career, and will need every effort by both the management and men in order to meet it. It presents an opportunity which we may never have again to establish an unassailable position in the American market. I am bound to say that the delivery dates which the distributors have specified leave no margin for any delays".'

Unfortunately, a few teething problems marred the early life of the Mark X to a small degree. There were problems with the radiators and there occurred a deterioration of the body to sub-frame rubbers.

Announced in 1963 and produced from 1964 until 1968, the S-Type saloon was a compromise heralded by the factory as 'the latest development of one of the world's most successful cars'. To call it a compromise may sound a little unfair because it was a very good car, inheriting a number of the better features from the models that sired it. It was basically a Mark II in shape and specification, with the following exceptions. Most importantly, it had the E-Type's independent rear suspension, which gave consider-

ably improved roadholding and comf[ort] over the Mark IIs, and for an increa[sed] outlay of only £200. It had the long[er] rear-end boot treatment along the li[nes] of the Mark X, giving an increase [of] 7 cu ft over the Mark II, and was sligh[tly] re-styled at the front. A flatter roof l[ine] and changes to the rear seats gave m[ore] head and leg room in the back.

Available in both 3.4 and 3.8 for[m] (but not with the 2.4 unit because of t[he] S-Type's extra three cwt) and priced [at] £1,669, and £1,758 for the larg[er]

1

2

90

ined version, the S-Type was a ppy compromise that sold steadily. It ved one motoring magazine to comnt that the car was 'outstanding value money, combining effortless high ed cruising for four people with really ssuring road manners'. The ride, as sult of the independent rear suspen-n was, they said, 'probably unexcelled any other European car'.

n 1963 Massimo, an Italian firm, ounced a 12-plug head for the E-pe. Little more is known about these

heads or whether many were produced, but the concern claimed 'a very considerable increase in power output', aided no doubt by the three Webers they also fitted!

In 1964 the E-Type matured a stage further with two major alterations and several smaller ones. Firstly, the 3.8 engine was replaced by a 4.2 version of the trusty old XK engine. The 4235 cc capacity was achieved by re-designing the block and resulted not in any greater power output, still quoted at 265 bhp

1 *An imposing car from any angle, the Mark X's bulbous sides now date the car somewhat* (J C) 2 *The S-Type, available in both 3.4 and 3.8 form, was a marriage of Mark 2 and Mark X ideas* (J C) 3 *Apart from adding the 4.2 engine in 1964, Jaguar silenced the only major criticism of the earlier E-Type with an all-synchromesh gearbox* (J C) 4 *Still looking as fresh as it did at its introduction, the Series I 4.2 had not yet suffered the constraints that were to come* (J C) 5 *The 4.2 Mark X was notable for its new Marles Varamatic Bendix power-steering, unique to Jaguar* (J C)

5

1

2

(gross) at 5,500 rpm (as opposed to 5,400 for the 3.8), but did achieve a significant improvement in torque, rising from 260 lbs/ft at 4,000 rpm to 283 lbs/ft at the same engine speed.

The other major alteration was long overdue, namely the fitting of an all-synchromesh gearbox. The slightly increased power which this absorbed was more than compensated for by the increased satisfaction on the road.

Outwardly the cars remained virtually unchanged, the only obvious way of identifying the new models being the small '4.2' on the rear. Inside, the cars had much improved seats with the bright aluminium fascia and transmission tunnel giving way to leather-finished items introduced in late 1963, and an alternator was also fitted. Gone was the old Kelsey-Hayes bellows-type brake servo, to be replaced by a Lockheed vacuum booster.

These changes resulted in a slight increase in weight, and prices increased to £1,896 for the open car and £2,032 for its closed sister. Production figures were 9,548 and 7,770 respectively.

In 1964 the Mark X was further developed with the enlarged engine of 4.2 litres being fitted, as with the E-Type. The exterior remained unchanged apart from the addition of a small '4.2' on the boot lid.

A new improved Borg-Warner automatic transmission was offered and the power steering came in for some attention with the adoption of the Marles Varamatic variable rate system. A manual version was still offered and the new gearbox, again shared with the sports car, was a considerable improvement. This was appreciated by motoring writers, who had been less than generous in their comments on the previous box. They also approved of the more efficient and controllable heating system.

With these all-round improvements the Mark X continued to be in great demand both at home and across the Atlantic. The detail improvements enabled it to be described as 'a large power-

1 *The larger-engined Mark X was enhanced by revised automatic transmission and Dunlop radial tyres (*J C*)* 2 *The 2 + 2 version of the E-Type lost a little of its line. This early car does not carry the chrome trim below the side window that was normally a distinguishing feature of the 2 + 2 (*J C*)* 3 *The 420 saloon's engine was fitted with two carburettors instead of three, and as a result developed 20 bhp less than its larger sister (*J C*)* 4 *The central slat to the radiator and chrome side moulding clearly distinguish this 420G (*J C*)*

ful, roadworthy and luxurious car able to transport five people and their luggage in great comfort over long distances'.

Interestingly, the Jaguar brochure for this model stated that 'the latest techniques and equipment for rustproofing and painting are utilized to ensure maximum body life and higher standards of finish.' This anti-corrosion treatment was hardly effective (as can be judged today), indicating that the body engineers still had a fair amount to learn in this department. The ravages of time have been far from kind to the Jaguar ranges of the 1950s and 1960s, as anyone restoring an example today is only too well aware.

Typical of Jaguar development activities, Norman Dewis, Jaguar chief tester, surprised his fellow motorists with an indecently fast Mark X. The bonnet was well and truly locked down, but it was rumoured that underneath, the engine had twice the normal number of cylinders. Could this be a sign of things to come?

The year 1966 saw a new model which further extended the E-Type's role and therefore its market. Until then, the E had been strictly a two-seater with the various limitations that had imposed on owners with families or other commitments. The introduction of a 2 + 2 model enabled two extra adults to be conveyed for short distances or two children to be carried indefinitely. This model, being rather longer, made the option of automatic transmission possible and increased demand from the United States, where a high proportion of motorists favour, if not expect such an option.

The 2 + 2 was lengthened by 9 inches, the roofline raised by 2 inches, the doors extended by 8½ inches, the frontal area increased by 5% and the weight by 2 cwt. Mechanically, the car was only altered to care for increased weight by minor changes to spring rates and damper rates, etc. Inevitably, performance suffered, with a top speed for the automatic version of only 136.2 mph, and it took 1.6 seconds longer to reach 60 mph from standstill.

In July 1966, much to many people's surprise, Sir William Lyons and Sir George Harriman of BMC (British Motor Corporation) announced that their companies would merge to form British Motor Holdings (BMH). Autonomy would be maintained and strength and security gained from unity. That was the theory.

Although it may seem a harsh judgement the 420, announced at Earls Court in October 1966, was merely an interim model. It was a further compromise along S-Type lines and can simply be described as an S-Type with Mark X frontal treatment and the 4.2 engine. It served to show the way the Lyons theme was developing with looks somewhat akin to the completely new saloon range that was to follow a couple of years later. But in spite of this it was not a bad car. One leading motoring magazine considered it to be 'a saloon that for a combination of speed, comfort and safety is as good as any in the world, regardless of cost'.

The following optional extras could be specified when ordering a 420: foglamps at £15 9s 9d the pair, power-assisted steering at £67 12s 1d, air-conditioning for £280 5s 0d, an electrically heated rear window for £18 8s 9d, a laminated windscreen at £6 9s 0d and wire sp[e] wheels at £43 0s 5d silver painted, £95 5s 2d chromium plated. All pri[ces] included purchase tax. The list c[on]cluded: 'Every effort is made to m[eet] individual requirements. The above [are] details extras most often requested'.

The large saloon displayed at Ea[rls] Court in 1966 was no longer a Mark [X] but a 420G. You would have be[en] forgiven for being a little perplex[ed] because outwardly they looked identi[cal] apart from a chrome strip down eit[her] side of the 420G with a small flasher u[nit] at the forward end of it, a bolder cent[re] slat to the grille and the substitution [of] small grilles for the previously fit[ted] spotlights. The price was increased [by] £81 to £2,237.

Inside the car, as a sop to the saf[ety]

1

2

agonists who were beginning to be …d, the dash top sprouted a thick pad-… roll, which incorporated a clock. … seats were slightly altered in an …t to improve lateral support, …use the front seat passengers had …ded to slide around on the vast …ight seats (which resembled those of …XKs) during spirited cornering. …erwise the car was unchanged.

…limousine model had also been pro-…ed during 1966. It had first been seen …Mark X form and continued in 420G …e. This varied only in that it had a …sion between the front and rear seats, …ocktail cabinet and larger picnic …es. It was claimed that the rear seat …one of the widest available and 'pro-…s ample lounging room for three full …adults'.

Jaguar were able to announce in 1966 that exports of postwar models to America now topped 200 million dollars in total value.

The Mark IIs became 240s and 340s in 1967, and the 3.8 model was deleted from the range. The so-called new models differed little from their predecessors. The concept was becoming a little dated by then, but it should be remembered that the original 2.4 was announced in 1955, so it is hardly surprising.

In the interests of economy, hide seats were discontinued, and the Mark II's spotlights gave way to small circular grilles first seen on the Mark Is. In an attempt to modernize the model slightly, the previous rather heavy double curvature bumpers were replaced by re-

designed single slimline examples.

Meanwhile the evolution of the E-Type took a further step with the introduction in October 1968 of the Series Two version of the Roadster, the fixed-head and the 2+2. The majority of changes were to the exteriors and were largely dictated by US Federal Safety Regulations, the bane of exciting cars.

The front was altered, with a larger bonnet intake (for the optional air-conditioning unit), raised wrap-round

1 The Mark X/420G limousine carried added refinements for extra privacy (J C) 2 Made for only one year, the 340 was now the only other version because the 3.8-litre engine had been dropped (J C) 3 The new slimmer bumpers of the 240 and 340 were an attempt to prolong the life of the ageing Mark 2s

1

2

bumpers, the disposal of the headlamp covers (actually carried out a little earlier on what are known as Series 1½ cars), the movement of the headlamps up and forward so that they protruded above the bonnet, breaking the smooth line, and larger combined sidelamp and flasher units. The rear suffered in a similar way, with again larger and higher wrap-round bumpers, much larger rear lamp units and a square number plate. The car also carried additional flashers on front and rear wings and de-eared spinners. In line with the regulations, the interior had minor changes, including the obligatory rocker switches.

Braking was considerably improved with a Girling system with three pistons at the front and two at the rear. Power steering was now an optional extra. To satisfy the US emission controls, models exported to those shores were fitted with Stromberg carburettors. This, together with the extra weight and the less clean shape, resulted in the performance being by E-Type standards pedestrian, with a top speed somewhere in the region of 125 mph.

The 2+2 shared all the changes of its sisters plus one further alteration. The rake of the large windscreen was increased by 7 degrees by moving the base forward virtually to the bonnet line. This helped the looks of the car a little, where it had previously looked too severe.

As with the XK150s in their day, the competition was catching up with Jaguar again, particularly in the States. Cars such as the De Tomaso Pantera, a combination of European chassis and styling with the brute force of an American Ford V8 engine, were showing up the E-type in stifled form. As a result, Jaguar needed to take a large technical and image-boosting step forward once more to keep ahead. And they had the answer up their sleeve.

1, 2, 3 *The Series II E-Type had to satisfy new safety regulations – and suffered in appearance as a result. Further sops to the safety protagonists were, amongst other things, the recessed door handles and rocker switches. The rear end suffered similarly, with its over-heavy treatment now dictated by regulations (J C)*

8 THE XJ RANGE

Unquestionable technical merit yielded high praise for the saloon range that replaced the ageing models in 1968, and the technical qualities were further enhanced by the sophisticated V12 engine fitted first to the final progression of the faithful E-Type. Its successor had initially to endure uniquely dark days for the company, but improved quality control, technical refinement, decisive inspired leadership and at last a replacement engine for the brilliant yet ageing XK unit, pulled the company through and spelt a highly optimistic future.

1

1968 Jaguar announced the XJ range, and again the company had a world-beater. It was and continued to be, more than 15 years later, widely acclaimed. The faithful and constantly developed XK engine was still used, and this was supplemented by the new V12 engine first used in the ultimate progression of the E-Type series in 1971. This sensational engine was very highly regarded and gave Jaguar the technical image just as the XK engine had done in 1948. A combination of pleasant styling and first-class engineering made these clearly the best Jaguars yet. The story had turned full circle, because just as the SSIs in their day were unkindly nicknamed 'the Bentleys of Wardour Street', so in the 1970s the motoring press compared the XJ12 with the Rolls Royce Silver Shadow ('The best in the world'), and asked, Which is the better? This was a tribute indeed to Sir William, who could see in the XJ the fulfilment of his original ambitions, from manufacturing stylish sidecars to arguably the finest production car in the world.

That the XJ range, in production for all of 18 years, was and continued to be a world-beater is too recent to need emphasising. As usual, the motoring press competed to express its extreme appreciation of the virtues of the new model introduced in 1968. One magazine stated that it was concerned

1, 2 Jaguar had another winner in the XJ6 and the major problem, as it had so often been, was meeting demand. Unquestionable technical merit impressed the motoring world, apart from the usual Lyons gift for styling seen once again in the XJ6 3 The XK engine was 20 years old but nobody would have known because it powered the XJ6 in silky silence 4 The V12 E-Type's major exterior change from the earlier models was the addition of a grille to enclose the famous mouth (J C)

4

that, being frustrated like many customers at having to wait months before being able to acquire an XJ6, the critics might make that frustration even greater for the customer by lengthening the waiting list still more. They went on to say that they felt that the car was 'closer to overall perfection than any other luxury car we have yet tested, regardless of the price'. It is interesting to note how often that phrase 'regardless of price' has been applied to Jaguar's products.

The new model, known simply as the XJ6, was offered with a choice of engines, either the familiar 4.2-litre or a new 2.8-litre version of the trusty XK design. Interestingly, Jaguar hinted of things to come when they made the significant statement in their press release at the launch, that 'Within the next two years, it is intended to introduce new additional power units into the range. The XJ6 has been designed to accept them and, therefore, in due course we plan to introduce further XJ models featuring the new engines'.

Construction, as with the previous models, was of the pressed steel monocoque variety with a massive central platform and stout scuttle structure. By thus concentrating the strength in the lower half of the body, the need for thick screen pillars and rear quarters was avoided.

Innovations as far as Jaguars were concerned were the provision of anti-dive geometry in the newly designed front suspension, and the fitting of new low profile, radial-ply tyres developed in conjunction with Dunlop. Another first for a Jaguar saloon was the choice of rack-and-pinion steering, power-assisted on the 4.2 and 2.8 de luxe models, and with that assistance as an optional extra on the basic 2.8-litre. Rear suspension was the usual independent set-up in a separate sub-frame.

Many safety features were built into the original design, including a collapsible steering column and independent front and rear hydraulic circuits for the Girling disc brakes, fitted all round.

Priced at £2,314 for the 4.2 manual gearbox with overdrive, and £1,797 for the basic 2.8-litre, these cars in the true Lyons tradition offered unbeatable value for money. The 32½ cwt did not help consumption, which averaged 15–17 mpg, but this was before the petrol rises and the economic depression.

In 1971 a manual 4.2 XJ6 supplemented the automatic versions. The car was somewhat quicker, but not many were made because automatic transmission was more popular for a car of this type.

The clutch on this model was particularly heavy, which did not endear it to drivers.

Braking for most purposes was more than satisfactory but the author recalls a high speed run in the late 1970s with Mike Barker of the Midland Motor Museum in their C-Type and Gordon Benbow in a Series 1 XJ6. I was in my XK140 Roadster. After about 30 miles of pretty hard motoring Benbow had to slacken off because the XJ's brakes were fading. This was ironic when you think of the XK's poor old drum brakes, but

it was probably explained by the fact t[hat] it was rather easier to scrub off speed [by] lateral cornering in the XK, and by [the] XJ's greater weight.

In mid-1969, the man whose co[n]tribution had been second in importa[nce] only to that of 'the Old Man', left [the] stage. Bill Heynes had achieved the ra[nk] of Vice-Chairman (Engineering) wh[en] he retired, and his country had rig[htly] rewarded him by honouring him wit[h a] CBE for his services to Jaguar.

For reasons of prestige, apart from [the] technical advantage, it was felt by Jag[uar]

1

2

the 1960s that they must have a [h]nmorous and technically sophisticated [.]ine to power the models of the 1970s [?] beyond, in the same way as they felt [?]the 1940s when they designed the [-]cylinder.

[T]he engineering brief for the new [?]ine called for a design offering a [?]ater degree of smoothness, silence [?] flexibility than the six, coupled to [?]ver and torque outputs which, in the [?]e engine's basic form, were required [?] be at least as good as the highest [?]res achieved by the XK unit. These

in their most advanced competition form produced approximately 325 bhp, and the V12 production engine came close to achieving this.

Like the development of the XK before it, the best ever achieved by the previous engine was made the starting point for the new. The parallels are fascinating.

The cylinders of the 12 were set in a V formation at an angle of 60 degrees with, in production, a single overhead cam per bank, although early versions designed with racing in mind had twin

1 *The greater length helped to offset the more cluttered front and rear treatment of the Series III E-Types* (J C) **2** *The centre-mounted V badge is the clue to the engine fitted to the XJ6 derivation, the XJ12* (J C) **3** *Like the XK150 in relation to the XK120, the V12E was thought by many to be a completely new model and is better regarded as such* (J C) **4** *To answer one of the few criticisms of the model, later XJs were available in long wheelbase form, adding four inches of legroom and* $1\frac{1}{2}$ *cwt* (J C) **5** *Continuing their long association, several police forces acquired squads of XJs, here in revised Series II form, for patrolling motorways* (J C)

4

overhead cams per bank. But eventually, cost, under bonnet space, noise and complexity decided the issue.

A bore of 90 mm and stroke of 70 mm gave a capacity of 5343 cc (326 cu in) which, with a compression ratio of 9:1, gave a gross power output of 314 bhp at 6200 rpm. An innovation at that time was the fitting of Lucas transistorized ignition. Aluminium was used extensively – the block was of aluminium in order to save weight.

Jaguar stated: 'In this engine we have provided quite a substantial reserve for capacity increases should the need arise (and) . . . it is relatively easy to derive a substantially smaller engine from the design'.

An entirely separate engine assembly line was set up for the production of the V12 engine and this was situated at the Radford plant. Total tooling-up costs were in the region of £3 million, with equipment for machining the heads accounting for some £700,000, and this at 1970 prices.

Assembly was carried out on an electrically driven 52-stage track, designed for ease of working, with vigorous inspection standards and final bench-testing before transfer to Browns Lane. Justifying the heavy capital outlay, Jaguar optimistically stated that 'the installation is geared to produce a future optimum of 1,000 major power unit components per 80-hour (two week) shift, and it is possible to utilize the equipment to produce alternative capacities and specifications. . . .'

It was no secret that Jaguar were working on a V12 engine in the 1960s. Its origins can be traced back to 1955 and the racing days when it was considered that more power would be needed to keep ahead of the opposition, so some drawings were made. As with the XK engine, it was designed for the saloon range and was fitted in the sports car as a 'production test bed'. It was destined for the XJ saloon, but first it was to be offered in the E-Type.

Externally the Series Three E differed considerably from its earlier sisters. A grille appeared at the front to replace the open mouth. Wheel arches were slightly flared to accommodate wider tyres and increased track. Only a 2+2 and a version known simply as 'open' were offered and the latter, although it had only two seats, shared the longer wheelbase chassis of the 2+2. This change allowed the open model also to be available with automatic transmission. The previously optional power steering was now standard and very necessary because of the extra weight of

these cars – 28.8 cwt for the Roadster and 29.5 cwt for the 2+2, an increase of nearly a quarter over the original Series One model. However, in spite of this weight disadvantage and the further cluttered shape, the V12 engine produced performance figures comparable to the early cars and were a considerable improvement on the interim models.

Prices of the new models were in the true Jaguar tradition, the Roadster being listed at £3,123 and the closed version at £3,369. It is interesting to note in

these inflation-beset days that the Roadster had increased in price from 1961 1971, a period of 10 years, by £1,29 some 70%.

Inevitably, the XJ12 eventua arrived, and the poor motoring journ ists, who only four years earlier had u all the superlatives they could beg, b row or steal now had to redouble th efforts. Some simply asked 'The m luxurious car in the world?', while oth stated it as a fact.

The V12 engine, already tried

1

2

ted in the Series Three E-Type was, mentioned, always destined for the ~~~on. Even so, the installation was not easy one. It was a very large engine, ecially with all the ancillaries dictated comfort and regulations, and this left cious little space to spare in the ~ine compartment. This resulted in problem of how to dissipate surplus t. A series of modifications to the ~ling system, including a newly igned cross-flow radiator, solved the ~blem. Such was the thoroughness of

the Jaguar engineers that a fan was fitted to cool the battery in case of high ambient temperatures.

Apart from the fitting of ventilated front discs, a different grille and dif-

ferent badges, the car was largely the same as the six-cylinder version.

The V12 engine gave the XJ12 a top speed of around 140 mph and meant that this was the fastest production four-

1 The interior of the Series II XJs demonstrated that in spite of modern ergonomics Jaguar still favoured good traditional quality (J C) 2 The two-door pillarless treatment of the XJCs particularly suited the model (P. Porter) 3 With both side windows down, the Coupé was a most attractive, stylish and almost sporting car (P. Porter) 4 The XJS

undergoing the extensive development testing that is an ever increasing part of a new model's gestation period (N. Dewis) 5 The newly announced XJS leads a parade of racing cars round the streets of Birmingham – no prize for guessing which of Jaguar's distributors it belonged to (J C)

4

seater in the world in 1972. And the price for this privilege was just £700 more than that of the XJ6, making a total of £3,672.

In the pre-petrol crisis world, demand was very heavy and the consumption, which could be as high as 12 mpg, was irrelevant to many people. The waiting list was so long that Jaguar's own advertising used cartoons with captions such as 'Welcome to the first XJ12 up our street'.

Jaguar had acquired Daimler in 1960 and now indulged in that questionable art of badge engineering. In late 1972 a Vanden Plas version of the Daimler XJ12 known as the Double Six, was announced, at a cost of £5,363. The significance of this model was that the wheelbase was increased by 4 inches. The two Jaguar saloons became available in this long-wheelbase form, whence they were known as XJ6Ls and XJ12Ls.

In 1972 Sir William Lyons, at the age of 71, bowed out, some 50 years after those humble beginnings and ardent ambitions. Lofty England stepped up to become his successor as Chairman and Chief Executive, and Lyons took the honorary title of President.

Towards the end of 1973, at the Frankfurt Show, the factory announced new improved versions of the popular XJs, and these were christened the Series Two.

The V12-engined saloon was no longer available on the short 108.8-inch wheelbase, but only in the 112.8-inch body. The 2.8 was dropped from the home market and from then on was available only in certain continental markets where taxation or insurance made it viable. The 4.2 version now had the ventilated front discs and sculptured wheels fitted previously to the V12 only. The new cars also featured a single-tube oil cooler, a brake pressure differential warning actuator and a revised exhaust system that eliminated the flexible pipe section. Anti-intrusion barriers welded into the doors provided protection designed to meet legal requirements anywhere in the world. Improved sound deadening on the front bulkhead included the elimination of all grommets, a full-width asbestos sheet attached to the front of the bulkhead and the interior face of the bulkhead; and the footwells and transmission hump had a moulded sound-absorbing material that consisted of Olfield bitumen and cotton felt and Hardura PVC foam with a loaded PVC surface. Dedication indeed to the continuous quest for more silence!

The interior came in for considerable re-vamping, with a complete new dash layout. The confusing tumble or rocker switches had given way to a more modern push-push variety and there was a general re-grouping of instruments.

Externally the new models had detail changes that made them look quite different. In order to satisfy North American safety requirements for 1974 the front bumpers were raised 4 inches to a height of 16 inches. This necessitated a new smaller grille above the bumper a below a rectangular grille with horizo tal bars that concealed the new oil cool The rear came in for less attenti Lighting for the rear number plate v moved from below the plate to abov and formed a single chromium-pla metal casting with the boot lid lock new heating system, the fitting of pov steering, a heated rear window a

inated windscreen as standard com-
ed the main changes. The long
eelbase versions also had electrically
rated windows and head restraints as
idard equipment.

he various improvements enabled
uar's to keep abreast if not ahead of
ir main rivals, notably the BMWs and
rcedes of Germany, and executives
rywhere continued to covet the

model. But at the factory, management
and workforce were going through turbulent times. A year after Lofty took the
helm, Lord Stokes appointed outsider
Geoffrey Robinson as Managing Director and several months later, to the disappointment of many, Lofty retired. In
mid-1975 Robinson resigned over the
infamous Ryder Report and its suicidal
proposed submersion of Jaguar's auto-

nomy and very identity.

At the same time as Jaguar released the
Series Two saloons, they also announced
a new model, the XJ Coupé. Mechanically, and in most other respects identical to the saloons, the Coupés had one
major difference and it was a striking one
– namely, the cars had two doors instead
of four, and pillarless construction. The
doors were enlarged by 8 inches and the
side windows, electrically operated,
could be completely lowered from sight
thus giving a very sporting appearance.
This was further enhanced by a neat
vinyl roof.

Based on the short wheelbase body,
the car was still a full four-seater, with
access gained to the rear by tilting the
front seats forward.

To make good any torsional stiffness
lost through the omission of the central
pillars, the rear quarters were increased
in thickness and reinforcing beams
inside the body were provided. In fact,
production did not begin for a couple of
years because of teething problems with
torsional rigidity, and effective operation
and sealing of the windows.

The company's advertising claimed,
'That comparatively rare person, in
whom a spirit of individuality remains
strong, will find freedom of expression
in the dignified, exclusive yet vivacious
performance of these superb cars'. This
was quite reminiscent of the early Swallow days. Certainly the Coupés were
more distinctive than the saloons, and
their relative exclusivity was ensured
when the company decided to concentrate on the long wheelbase saloons.
This decision killed off the Coupé, the
V12 version of which, with fuel injection, was capable of around 145 mph.

In the mid-1970s the company
introduced fuel injection for the V12 XJs
for reasons of economy. For similar
reasons the old faithful 3.4 litre,
although in rather different form, was
re-introduced for the four-door saloons.
In 1975 the 3.4, at £4,795, cost some
£342 less than the 4.2-litre.

When the XJS was at last announced
in 1975, the critics were divided in their
opinions. This was a unique situation for
a Jaguar sports car. But there was a problem – it was no longer a sports car. Some
complained that it lacked the dramatic
appeal and sporting pretensions of the
XK120 and E-Type before it; others
claimed that this did not matter, that it

*The range for the early 1980s posed alongside
an RAF Vulcan (J C)*

was a high-speed luxury car appropriate to the 1970s and 1980s. Nobody tried to call it a sports car, and nobody denied that it was technically superb. Really it was the culmination of a trend away from the wind-in-the-hair extrovert sports car first seen in 1948, a trend continued by the less sporting XK150 to the more sophisticated E-Type to the even more sophisticated V12E. What would those diehards who complained at the wind-up windows of the XK150 Roadster say when they observed that those of the XJS were electrically powered?

Technically the XJS was closely based on the XJ saloons, with similar monocoque construction, and the same front anti-dive suspension and independent rear suspension, although both front and rear were stiffened with a new rear anti-roll bar of 14 mm and a larger front one. This resulted in a firmer ride more in keeping with the car's sporting pretensions instead of the slightly spongy feel of the saloons. The power steering had been geared down for more feel, taking just three turns from lock to lock. The engine was the familiar V12 unit but fitted with Lucas fuel injection. For transmission you had a choice between the usual manual four-speed box or Borg Warner three-speed Model 12 automatic. Braking was very adequately taken care of by the 11.18-inch diameter ventilated discs with four piston calipers at the front and the inboard 10.38-inch diameter discs with two piston calipers at the rear, along with vacuum assistance and dual hydraulic lines.

People were also divided on their views of the styling. Certainly the influence of the safety fanatics could be detected immediately and clearly in the heavy black impact-absorbing rubber bumpers, which were mounted to Menasco struts that acted like shock absorbers to withstand the compulsory 5 mph impact. Creature comforts were well cared for, with air conditioning standard, and reclining front seats with separate squab centre section for lateral support. The interior was trimmed throughout in flame-retardant materials and no fewer than 18 mechanical and safety functions were monitored through a bank of coloured lights. Red lights indicated major faults, such as brake failure, and amber lights denoted secondary faults such as brake bulb failure.

With a top speed of 150 mph, the ability to cruise in almost total silence, with a consumption of 15–18 mph, excellent road manners and great safety, the XJS could well be, technically at least, what the advertising script claimed

– 'The pinnacle of Jaguar evolution'.

Jaguar testing and development has long been extensive and exhaustive, but never more so than today, with the increased complexity of the many world-wide technical regulations to be met. This has resulted in a greatly extended embryonic period, to the frustration of many. Overseeing the physical testing of all cars since 1952 had been Norman Dewis. He had been involved with both racing development and the production side, to say nothing of the high-speed publicity runs and the driving of the racing models to the events.

Early in 1979 the XJ saloons were given a facelift – in other words, the body was modernized. This was achieved by subtle restyling rather than major surgery. The roofline was raised at the rear to give a lighter look and more headroom, and the inevitable heavy black bumpers incorporating front indicators and rear fog lights were grafted on. The

design, re-tooling and production co amounted to £7 million, which is int esting to compare with the £1 milli needed some 24 years earlier to co pletely develop the small 2.4-li saloon. Uniquely for the company, outside design studio was retained Jaguar to advise on this XJ revamping

New flush door handles, an optio wash/wipe device for the headlamps, outer of which now incorporated sidelights, a new grille, a new rear lig cluster and number plate lamp were features of the Series III.

On the mechnical side, the remained unchanged, but the 3.4 and could be had with a five-speed gear b (ex-Rover suitably modified) or Model 65 Borg Warner automatic be The 4.2 was fitted with Lucas fuel inj tion and the inlet valves were increas to $\frac{7}{8}$-in, the same as the D-Type hea resulting in a useful increase of 30 bh

The interior had deep-pile carpeti

1

2

greater luxury and even greater
nd deadening, and one magazine
mented, 'Other cars are quiet but
uars (and Rolls Royces) are silent'.
nt seats came in for attention with the
ption of an adjustable lumbar sup-
t system, and an optional extra was
electrical height control of the
ver's seat. Other optional extras
luded a cruise control device, an elec-
ally operated sliding roof, and many
re minor items.

By the year 1984, the basic XJ 3.4
oon cost just £11,188, or £11,017-10s-
more than the original basic Swallow
en two-seater; but one can hardly
npare the two, to put it mildly. While
Swallow was a good little car of its
e, the latest XJs could openly com-
e for all-round excellence with any
er car then produced. It is a matter
rom simply being imitators of style
the company's youth to becoming
ders in mass production engineer-

ing sophistication in the fullness of
maturity; and from offering a naïve but
pretentious product to providing a 'full-
bodied' one, par excellence.

In 1980 a saviour in the form of John
Egan arrived as full-time Chairman of
Jaguar. During the period following
Robinson's departure in 1975, the company had been 'barely' run by a series of
committees with several virtually nom-
inal figureheads. Apart from Bob
Knight's brief spell, all the chiefs had
been outside men.

Egan, however, brought fresh hope.
Here was a man with respect for the past
and belief in the future. He brought
an intelligent coherence once more to
Jaguar's existence. Gradually he tackled
the problems, concentrating particularly
on the wayward quality that had sadly
been a part of the 1970s. He rekindled
Jaguar's autonomy, rebuilding the image.
And slowly the company returned to
profitability. Exports, particularly to the

States, began to match the results of
earlier years, and the company again
became Jaguar Cars Ltd.

A few days after his 80th birthday in
1981, Sir William was quoted in the
Birmingham Evening Mail as believing
that Jaguar's only hope was to 'go it
alone'. Still President, he stated, 'I think
it's a very good idea to sever Jaguar links
with BL. Jaguar should be a separate
entity, and I think Sir Michael Edwardes
is leaning that way.' Lyons believed that

1 *Perhaps the best view of the high-speed executive express that visibly reflected American
safety regulations in its front and rear treatment (*J C*)* 2 *The controversial rear end treatment of the XJS. Whatever the styling, you
could travel at high speed and in unprecedented
silence (*P. Porter*)* 3 *Soon after its introduction with automatic transmission only, the XJS
was offered with the V12E's four-speed manual
box (*J C*)*

top management at Jaguar was in good hands. 'They are making a success of things and restoring the company to its original standing.'

In November 1982 *The Sunday Times Business News* published a full-page article detailing Jaguar's recovery and dramatically increased export business with the headline: 'Jaguar Climbs out of the Pit'.

Fuel economy became increasingly important in the late 1970s and early 1980s, following the petrol crises and dramatic increase in prices. Mindful of this, Jaguar engineers turned their attention to reducing consumption of the six- and particulary the thirsty twelve-cylinder engines. As a result, they introduced a new version of the latter engine termed the HE, the initials standing for High Efficiency.

The modifications consisted of the application of the Fireball combustion chamber principles, invented by Swiss engineer Michael May, and used for the first time in a production car. Jaguar engineers had spent five years perfecting the May principles to suit the demands of a production engine. The secret of the design lay in the split-level combustion chamber arrangement, with the inlet valve set into a shallow collecting zone and the exhaust valve set higher up within the bath-tub type combustion chamber, which also housed the sparking plug. A swirl-inducing ramped channel connected the two areas. The resulting swirl characteristics ensured rapid and complete burning of very lean fuel mixtures.

The XJS HE, now claimed by the factory to be the fastest automatic transmission production car in the world, reminds us of the claims made for the XK120 when it was announced. The mechanical changes improved consumption from an urban figure of 12.7 mpg to 15.6 mpg, with 27 mpg at 56 mph and 22.5 mpg at 75 mph, with a top speed of 155 mph. The coupé had a different bumper arrangement, with an element of chrome lightening the effect of the large black appendages. A tapered double coach-line distinguished the side aspect of the new model and the bonnet sprouted a flat circular jaguar's head badge not dissimilar from that of the XK120s. Five-spoke alloy wheels, veneer fascia, extensive use of Connolly hide, Dunlop D7 tyres on 6½-in rims and a new Philips 990 micro-computer stereo radio-cassette unit completed the updating.

The twelve-cylinder saloons received the same HE engine, the title therefore of XJ12 HE, alloy wheels, electrically

operated sun roof and door mirrors, and a headlamp wash/wipe.

On 12th October 1983 Jaguar announced additional new models but, in the longer term of more significance, a new engine. The model had been rumoured for some time and was an open version of the XJS, the Cabriolet. The engine was the new six-cylinder, the eventual successor to the perennial XK unit some 35 years after the latter's first appearance. The XK continued to power the 3.4 and 4.2 saloons but the new engine was obviously intended for the XJ40 range of saloons scheduled for introduction in the mid-1980s. Interestingly, following established Jaguar practice, the new engine was introduced in a low-volume sports model first.

Plans to produce a three-quarter scale 3.5 litre V-8 version of the V12 engine, thereby enabling the unit to be built on the same production line thus keeping capital investment to a minimum, had to be dropped when it was found the engine in this form suffered from secondary out of balance forces. The fitting of a balance

shaft cured this but precluded using V12 lines, so it was abandoned in 197

Further experiments included building of half a V12 in the form o slant six cylinder. This engine of 2.6 l capacity was found to be lacking power and any increase in stroke ma the engine too high to machine on V12 line. Next a V12 unit was bu spurred by competitive thoughts, 1972 with four-valves-per-cylin heads based mainly on the gr experience Wally Hassan and Ha Mundy had gained whilst build Grand Prix engines at Coventry Clin with this configuration. This eng which developed 630 bhp was not p severed with as competition id receded but the lessons learnt were prove valuable.

In 1974 a four-valve version of the unit was built with a view to produc the unit on the existing six-cylin engine facilities. The resultant 3.8 u proved satisfactory but the constraint a 30-year-old design, the need greater economy and the work be

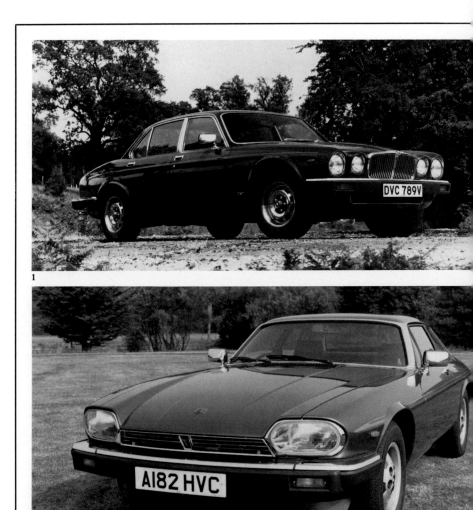

1

2

e with the May head on the V12 all
nted against this plan. Thus the
ior decision had to be taken to lay
vn a new engine assembly line. This
ision gave the designers a much freer
d, the only proviso being that the
y head for the new engine had to be
e to be produced on the same line as
V12 May head; thus the cylinder
e centres necessarily had to be the
e on both engines. It was decided to
ld two versions of the six, one with
May head for economy and one with
24 valve head for performance.

The new engine introduced in the XJS
d a bore and stroke of 91 × 92 mm, giv-
a capacity of 3,590 cc, and with the
valve head developed 225 bhp at
00 rpm. This compared with the XK
t in 1980's guise giving 162 bhp in 3.4
e form and 205 bhp in 4.2 litre form.

The massively ribbed, deep skirted
minium block extended well below
crankshaft which ran in seven main
rings. The extensive use of light
ys meant that the new AJ6 (as it was

called) was some 25–30 per cent lighter
than the 4.2 XK unit. Other features
included Lucas digital electronic fuel
injection and a Lucas constant energy
ignition system. For reasons of height
the engine was inclined 15° from the
vertical.

The AJ6 was developed by Hassan
and Mundy's successors, Jim Randle,
Engineering Director, and Trevor
Crisp, Chief Engineer (Power Units).
The capital investment required amounted to over £21 million with £6 million
alone for the new transfer line for
machining the cylinder blocks. Jaguar
stated that this new line had a capacity
of one thousand blocks a week.

As stated the AJ6 engine was introduced in the XJS in both the Coupé version
and the new open Cabriolet. The 3.6
Coupé was priced at £19,250 and offered
with 5 speed Getrag box giving the car
a much more sporty feel. Top speed was
145 mph and 60 mph could be reached
in 7.6 seconds. Consumption was said to
be around 25 mpg for mixed driving

conditions. Externally the main distinguishing feature was a reprofiled bonnet with long bulge to accommodate the
new engine.

The Cabriolet shared the same
mechanical specification and new bonnet. Internally, however, there were
changes for this was a two seater with the
area behind the seats used for luggage
storage only. The XJ-SC 3.6 was not an
open car in the traditional 'convertible'
sense but had what has come to be
known as a 'targa' top. Fixed cantrails
and a centre bar allowed various options.
The roof consisted of two interlocking
panels which could be removed together
or singly, being stored in an envelope in
the boot. To the rear could be fitted
either a hard-top type heated rear
window or a double-skinned folding
hood.

The new shape – though more pleasing to the eye – was obviously a little less
efficient in the windstream as top speed
was quoted at the slightly more modest
figure of 142 mph.

1 *Subtle restyling and the inevitable impact
bumpers easily distinguish the Series III XJ
models, belying the fact that the XJ was more
than 10 years old (*J C*)* 2 *The later XJS HE
was improved in appearance by the addition of
a thin chromed top bumper blade and 'cheese-
cutter' wheels (*J C*)* 3 *Marque name changes
led to partial dropping of the Daimler name and
this model, the V12 Saloon, became the Jaguar
Sovereign HE (*J C*)* 4 *The XJSC 3.6 Cabriolet with both roof panels removed and the
optional folding rear window down is a more
stylish machine. Note the discreet bonnet bulge
to accommodate the new AJ6 engine (*J C*)*

9 THE LEGEND REVIVED

After several delays the crucial XJ40 saloon, the successor to the evergreen XJ6 range, finally appeared in 1986. Demand was keen until a strong pound in the late eighties hampered sales in the important US market, and profits were wiped out. In an age of automotive giants, Jaguar was but a charismatic minnow and the American big fish fought to swallow the British company. Though it would no longer be independent, undeniable industrial logic at least pointed to a safe and strong future for this proud name.

1

h a highly favourable dollar/sterling
tionship persisting through the
y and mid-eighties, company
unes continued to be rebuilt. De-
d remained strong for the Series
and took the urgency out of launch-
its successor. Egan continued his
e for improved quality and the P.R.
artment concentrated on building
image around Egan and putting
ss the improved quality and resul-
reliability.

uriously in the States the Series III
perceived as a new car, and its style
anced it from the more utilitarian
manic box-like shape of its main

imported rivals. However, whether
they lacked style or not, these rivals had
made tremendous inroads into the market and though Jaguar's sales made a
dramatic recovery year-on-year in per-
centage terms, they were still way
behind the annual sales of Mercedes-
Benz, B.M.W. and Porsche, even taken
individually, and miniscule in comparison with the total market.

Jaguar had a great deal of catching up
to do having sunk so low whilst
Mercedes had made constant progress
throughout Jaguar's troubled times.
Coventry production had taken a dive
from the 1974 figure of 26,632 to a

miserable 15,011 in 1981. The important home market sales which had
been 14,444 in the former year plum-
meted to an insignificant 5688 in the
latter year. However, by '84 total sales
had shown a considerable improvement
to 33,404 and this upward trend was
continuing.

The gestation period of the XJ6's
successor, codenamed XJ40, was a long
and rather tortuous one. It actually
commenced as far back as 1972, when
Lofty England had the job of persuad-
ing the British Leyland Board that the
company was capable of producing a
new model and that the funds should be
allocated for such.

It is ironic that Jaguar should have to
go cap in hand to Leyland to seek the
money for, as Bob Knight ruefully
recalls, 'between 1969 and 1974, Jaguar
had contributed £24m positive cash
flow which, in the money of the times,
was a lot. That was, in effect, bullion
that was hauled over the gates at
Browns Lane and poured down the
bottomless pit at Longbridge. This
money could have made all the difference to Jaguar because it could have
been used to provide Jaguar with a new
body assembly shop and paint shop,
and would have allowed us to pay
decent salaries to attract, and keep,
engineers. Jaguar would have been
transformed by '74.'

A succession of drawings and models
were made as various people tried to fill
the 'styling vacuum' left by Sir William
Lyons. Following one of the greatest
practitioners of the art of automotive
styling was, quite obviously, no simple
matter.

Geoffrey Robinson, during his brief
tenure in office, had consulted the
Italians and Pininfarina, Bertone and

1 *During the long and difficult development
period the XJ saloon replacement underwent,
a 'buggy' was built to thoroughly test the major
new suspension assemblies on the pavé.* (Jaguar
Cars) 2 *After several false starts, the new
saloons, codenamed XJ40, finally appeared in
October, 1986 and were generally very well
received.* (Philip Porter) 3 *In the United
States the new XJ40s, which officially perpe-
tuated the name XJ6, were launched in
mid-1987, after a careful build-up of production initially for the British and European
markets.* (Philip Porter)

Guigaro had all submitted full size models, but they lacked the essential style. Meanwhile, as Jaguar sales were falling due to appalling quality, the British Leyland management totally misread the situation and insisted the style of the new car should ape the plain Germanic creations that were enjoying a vogue.

Throughout this traumatic period of changing top management, one true Jaguar man fought harder than anyone else and kept the company alive. Bob Knight used all his considerable intellectual ability and engineering prowess to resist, as far as he could, the suicidal moves towards centralisation and complete loss of autonomy and identity.

Though pre-eminent as an engineer rather than a manager, he was rewarded when Sir Michael Edwardes arrived in the nick of time to restore sanity to the crumbling empire, and appointed him Managing Director of Jaguar. Thus was Knight able to influence the external design of the XJ40 and steer it back towards a shape that the public would perceive to be a Jaguar.

He describes himself as a reluctant stylist and, although responsible for the final shape, insists that he was, and is, far from happy with it.

Thus when Egan arrived on the scene, he inherited not only a styled car but also a team that had largely been put together by Knight, who sadly chose to leave shortly after.

With Knight's departure, Jim Randle, who was something of a protégé of his, was elevated and took on the herculean task of finalising the mechanical design and overseeing the development of the XJ40. As stated earlier, Jaguar sales were buoyant in the mid-eighties and this allowed the engineers much-needed time to refine the car to Jaguar's exacting standards.

In many ways the hardest task was to match, let alone exceed, the existing XJ range both in terms of style, and ride and refinement. With Jaguar being, in effect, a one-model company, it was vital for the very survival of the marque that the XJ40 should be a success. A series of styling clinics were held around the world and confirmed that the shape was acceptable, but the Americans, thankfully, rebelled at the thought of a plastic interior for a Jaguar, and an eleventh hour exercise was instigated to add the British craftsmanship for which Jaguars have always been famous.

Whilst prototypes were covering a much-vaunted total of $5^{1}/_{2}$ million miles in all extremes of climate, the

transformation in company fortunes had been such that the Conservative Government made the decision to float Jaguar as a separate entity from its infanticidal parent, or to use the popular jargon, it was to be privatized.

Offered at £1.65 each, the shares were over-subscribed by a factor of nearly ten, such was the euphoria surrounding Jaguar's charismatic return from the dead.

Sir William had had little to do with 'his' company during the dark days but in the early eighties he began to be a little involved once more. Egan consulted him and genuinely sought his advice. Furthermore, he visited the Styling Department on occasions and made some pertinent contributions.

On February 8th, 1985 Sir William Lyons, then in his eighty-fourth year, passed away. He had founded a minute company and retired from an empire. His styling flair and business acumen were legendary in the true sense of an over-used word. It is very sad that his son was so tragically killed and that he

did not have an heir whom he co imbue with the same extraordi qualities. Thankfully, he saw company become, once more, pr independent and successful.

Newly privatised and in unfette charge of their destiny once more, Jaguar management were able to d the introduction of the XJ40 and launch was postponed several tir The P.R. line was that the existing was selling so well there was no hu The reality was that there were se problems that needed to be overcon

One of these was the refinemen the AJ6 engine. Introduced in the X the unit had come in for some ha words from the press who, inevita found it compared unfavourable v the V12. Effort was expended tightening manufacturing toleran and a further direct comparison beca possible from July, 1985 when Cabriolet became available with 12-cylinder engine.

For the sum of £26,995, 150 r motoring was once more possible ir

1

2

Jaguar. With its Lucas-Bosch [Dig]ital Electronic fuel injection the car [coul]d attain a speed of 60 mph in seven [seco]nds with all the smoothness for [whi]ch the superb engine was famous.

[In] October, 1986 Jaguar finally took [the] plunge and amidst much euphoria [and] razzmatazz, replaced the XJ6 with [the] XJ6, for such was the new car to be [kno]wn. A trifle confusing though it may [be, i]t was reasoned that the name had an [aura] about it that it would be unwise [not] to capitalise upon.

[T]hough not radically different in [shap]e, the car was totally different [und]er the skin. Considerable attention [had] been paid to making the car of far [fewer] panels and employing more [com]plex, larger pressings. This assisted [the] twin aims of reducing weight and [imp]roving productivity. A new rear [susp]ension was developed by Randle [and] colleagues employing a unique [pen]dulum arrangement and moving the [brak]es outboard.

[A]s many of the faults which justifia[b]led to the appalling reputation for unreliability had emanated from the electrical system, considerable effort was expended on moving a stage nearer the seemingly elusive multi-plexing that has been threatened for so long. Employing a system called low-current earth line switching, connectors of a much higher standard, and up to seven on-board microprocessor controlled systems, the engineers believed that they had made a major advance.

Apart from the 3.6 litre version of the more refined AJ6 engine, a 2.9 litre variant was also offered. With its Getrag manual gearbox and firmer new suspension, the XJ40 felt quite a fast and sporting car, as the journalists who were invited to Scotland to try the car prior to the launch found. The fast, quiet roads suited the car and admirably displayed its sporting qualities.

The 2.9 was naturally rather less vivid and only marginally more economical. In automatic form it was rather disappointing and it was not exported to the States, where the stifling effect of the emission control equipment, blunted the performance of the 3.6. However, with 55 and 65 mph speed limits one barely noticed the difference.

Three levels of model were offered and known as the XJ6, the Sovereign and the Daimler, successively offering a higher level of appointment and sophistication.

The reaction was generally favourable from press and public alike. There were some who argued that Jaguar should have been less conservative, but this would have been a risky policy. Certainly the public were not slow to place their orders, and Jaguar were once more in the happy situation of having long waiting lists.

The V12 did not appear in the XJ40 because it had been decided that such a thirsty engine would be unacceptable in the later eighties and beyond. However, with B.M.W. about to announce such an engine and the rumours suggesting that Mercedes-Benz would in time do the same, Jaguar could hardly drop theirs. Thus the venerable Series III continued alongside what one might, unofficially, entitle the Series IV, whilst plans were hastily made to 'shoe-horn' the V12 into a long wheelbase version of the new shell.

Production continued to increase with a figure of 41,437 being achieved in 1986 despite the model changeover. In the same year John Egan's successes were rewarded with a knighthood and the company received the Queen's Award for Export Achievement for the third successive year.

1   The 'new' XJ6s were fitted with the AJ6 engine in either 2.9 or 3.6 litre form, although only the latter would be available in Jaguar's most important market, namely, the States. (Philip Porter)   2   With the Series III XJ12 continuing alongside the new car and XJ-S sales steadily improving, the healthy demand for the XJ40 allowed Jaguar to increase annual production to new heights. (Philip Porter)   3   In 1988 the 'skeleton' roof of the XJ-S Cabriolets was finally removed and the XJS became available in full convertible form. (Jaguar Cars)   4   In spite of the price tag of £36,000 demand for the XJS V12 Convertible was considerable and helped to further improve sales of the XJ-S range, which by the late eighties was accounting for roughly a third of total production. (Jaguar Cars)

Roger Putnam, who had succeeded Neil Johnson as Sales and Marketing Director, had been concentrating his efforts on extracting the dealers from the multi-franchise BL dealerships and appointing new Jaguar-dedicated outlets. Together with the new 'The Legend Grows' theme to the advertising, the solus dealers helped to foster the new image and depreciation of secondhand Jaguars became less dramatic, an important factor in selling new cars.

In May 1987 the company celebrated sixty years of car manufacture and, with the launch of the XJ40 in the States, production continued to climb ever higher. A few months later further milestones were passed with the announcement that 100,000 V12 engines and 50,000 XJSs had been produced.

Whilst the stylists were working on a more major update of the XJS, several mechanical changes were made for the 1988 models. Henceforth the 3.6 litre engine would only be available in the coupe version of the XJS, with the option of either manual or the recently introduced ZF automatic transmission. With revisions to the steering and suspension, the car was given a more sporting nature.

The Cabriolet lived on in V12 engined form only, though this model's days were numbered as well.

In October, 1987 came the stockmarket crash and Jaguar's shares, which from a flotation price of 165p had reached a high of around 630p, fell back dramatically, and failed to recover, hovering around the 260p mark for most of 1988.

Things were becoming a little tougher for Jaguar and the press were starting to tarnish the new image. Questions were beginning to be asked about quality and whether the vital reliability was really as good as it was vaunted to be. In the States the vogue for imported cars seemed to be on the wain but, above all, the pound had become uncomfortably strong against the dollar for Jaguar's liking.

The company's over-dependence on the US market led to a dramatic fall in profits. When sterling had been weak, and even looked like reaching parity with the dollar, Jaguar had been almost minting it. With the pound's recovery to the 1.80 region, profits slumped with every cent upwards costing Jaguar's bottom line £3m in annual profits.

It is interesting to reflect that Lyons never trusted the American market and in spite of strong demand and constant requests from his colleagues, never attempted to satisfy more than a proportion of that demand. He preferred to spread his risks and ensure full order books. It is ironic that when he retired in 1972 with long waiting lists for the XJ6 and XJ12, prices were soon increased to balance supply and demand, and production was increased by starting a nightshift with the result that quality suffered from the lack of skilled labour. Overnight, and unforeseen, the first of the fuel crises erupted and the company was exposed.

It is also ironic that the company should choose in the eighties to trust the market that Lyons was always so wary of. Just as Lyons learnt from some bad experieces, it is to be hoped that the Jaguar management applies the lessons. Indeed in the late eighties, they once again concentrated on building up the home market, Europe and the rest of the world.

Against this sadly gloomy background, the delightful XJS Convertible was launched. Undoubtedly the best looking XJS yet, the Converti-ble was available in V12 form only.

The small firm of Lynx, who known for their work with D-types, been steadily producing a trickle convertibles for some while Jaguar's American company, unable wait for Jaguar's version, had a arranged a U.S. conversion, but fina Jaguar introduced their own. It taken time for the project invol pretty extensive re-engineering in attempt to eliminate the pereni problem of scuttle shake, with adding excessive weight. The price having no solid roof, but considera more style, was some £36,000.

In early '88 a move that was thou to have considerable long-term sign cance took place when Jaguar and GK the massive engineering group, form a joint company entitled Vent Pressings Limited to manufacture major body pressings.

A few months later another jc venture was set up, this time with TV to form Jaguarsport. The intention to develop, manufacture and mar

1

2

114

performance and sporting deriva-
s of the range. This was surely a
d move for apart from satisfying
e markets, the resultant image
st could only benefit the image as a
le. For some time it had been the
of the sales team to lower the
rage age of the Jaguar owner to
er that of its rivals, which were
eived to be more sporty and trendy,
the racing successes certainly assis-
that aim.
uring the eighties the Engineering
artment grew dramatically. Tradi-
lly a very small team had designed
developed the range of models, but
ems in this day and age firms need
army of engineers to face the
easing complexity of modern motor
and regulations spawned by self-
aining bureaucracies.
o house this growing team, Jaguar
ired an ex-Talbot factory at
tley and commenced an extensive
rbishment. Here, like most other
s, they were working on such
lopments as four wheel drive, re-
active suspension systems, turbo-
charging of the six-cylinder engines,
various sizes of that engine and, of
course, the future models.

From all this research effort, sprang
the exciting XJ220 concept car that
stole the 1988 Motor Show. Built by
Jim Randle and a small team of enthusiasts, the car had not actually run, like
its predecessor of forty years before, the
XK120, but was estimated to reach the
dizzy heights of 200 mph plus.

Hefty deposits flooded in as prices of
£300,000 were mentioned but at that
stage Jaguar would not commit themselves as to whether it would be offered
for sale, albeit in a limited quantity, or
not. All they would say was that they
were handing the project to JaguarSport
for assessment.

1 *In 1988 a joint venture company was
formed between Jaguar Cars Ltd. and the
TWR Group to produce limited editions and
more sporting versions of the basic products.
Following the '88 Le Mans victory a special
version of the XJ40, named the JaguarSport
XJR 3.6, was launched at the NEC Motor
Show. (Jaguar Cars)* 2 *With production
expanding and the working conditions at the
Browns Lane plant becoming cramped and
dated, a new 'high-tech' Engineering Centre
was established on the opposite side of Coventry. (Jaguar Cars)* 3 *Forty years after the
XK120 had 'stolen' the 1948 Motor Show so
the startling new XJ220 had a similar effect in
1988. (Jaguar Cars)* 4 *The major difference,
apart from 40 years of mechanical and styling
evolution, was that this was a concept car
which was by no means certain to go into even
limited production. (Jaguar Cars)*

10 INTO THE NINETIES

For Jaguar the early nineties were dominated by the Ford takeover and resultant shake-up. Massive, fundamental reorganization resulted in genuinely improved quality which gradually translated into improving sales and, with a slimmed down workforce, the company once more returned to modest profits after heavy losses. After successive updating and refining of the models, an exciting new saloon range, which oozed traditional Jaguar style once more, was unveiled mid-decade.

1

2

ate '88 the first product of the new
uarSport concern was launched.
ing the production XJS V12 as a
s, it was modified in a variety of
s to produce a distinctively styled
ion which was entitled the XJR-S in
our of that year's Le Mans victory.
thermore the first 100 examples
e known as the *Celebration Limited
ion* model and featured a unique
ur and trim scheme, together with
nless steel treadplates on which the
d number of each car was shown.

In time for the 1988 Motor Show
JaguarSport also announced their
version of the XJ6 saloon. The XJR 3.6
was considerably altered visually with
colour keyed front and rear bumpers,
door sill mouldings and rear spoiler, to
give a more overtly sporty appearance.
The front grille was finished in matt
black and 'quad' style halogen headlamps were incorporated. Mechanically
the car was uprated to enhance handling
characteristics with special JaguarSport
dampers and anti-roll bar. The power

steering was modified to give greater
feel and distinctive wheels, together
with Pirelli P600 225/55ZR speed rated
tyres, were employed on this model
which cost £38,500.

At the Show Jaguar announced that
they were on target for total sales of
50,000 for the year and Roger Putnam,
the Sales & Marketing Director, stated
that, 'Overall we are achieving our
annual sales growth target of 10% and
on this basis we are planning to sell
around 55,000 cars next year'.

In this climate of optimism, when
cars like the Ferrari F40 were being sold
at vast premiums, it was announced that
the XJ220 supercar was to go into
limited production. Provided sufficient
orders were received, a minimum of 220
cars, and a maximum of 350, would be
built at a special new facility created for
designing, developing and building the
220 at Bloxham, near Banbury. There
were to be some major changes of
specification and overall size, but stylist
Keith Helfet was seconded to the new
JaguarSport facility to ensure that the
car retained its stunning good looks
that had so captivated the crowds at the
Motor Show. Rather than the V12
power unit, the car would be built with
a detuned version of TWR's V6 racing
engine in twin-turbocharged form. This
would make the car lighter, allow it to
be shortened and render the task of
meeting emission control regulations
rather easier. Furthermore, it was not to
be four-wheel drive like the prototype.

In spite of an initial price of £290,000,
which was exclusive of taxes but was to
be adjusted in line with inflation and
would finally become a UK total of
around £440,000, some 1,500 orders,
together with their £50,000 deposits,
were received within 48 hours, more
than 400 being from the UK alone.

*1 For the exciting XJR-S model, JaguarSport
fitted a bored out 6.0 litre version of the venerable
V12 engine from August 1989 and created a car
capable of nearly 160 mph. (J C) 2 With the
introduction of the new 4.0-litre XJ saloon,
JaguarSport naturally followed suit and offered
the XJR 4.0 which differed from the standard
version in having a higher compression ratio, a
Sport inlet manifold, a high lift camshaft and
remapped digital engine management system. (J
C) 3 Following Jaguar's sixth Le Mans win, the
opportunity was taken to celebrate with a limited
edition XJS V12 Coupé, badged 'LeMans V12'.
(J C) 4 In May, 1991 the XJS range came in for
its most fundamental revision since its original
launch back in 1975. Though not greatly altered
in appearance the rear side window treatment
was considerably improved. (J C)*

In March it was announced that 1988 turnover was £73m higher at £1,075m, but profits, due to unfavourable currency fluctuations, had halved to £47m. Production for the year had reached 50,603, some 1,400 ahead of the previous twelve months.

JaguarSport introduced an exciting replacement for the existing XJR-S, when they launched a 6.0-litre version. Though the 318 bhp produced by this unit was impressive the massive 362 lb. ft. of torque was claimed to be 'class-leading' and was 17% better than the 5.3-litre unit. The car was equipped with a Zytec sequential injection and digital ignition engine management system which had been developed from

Jaguar's Group C racing program Uprated springs and specially develo Dunlop uni-directional D40 rad allowed the power to be translated in 0–60 time of 6.5 seconds, a 0–100 t of 15.4 seconds and a maximum spee 158 mph. The *Urban* economy c worked out at just 12.0 mpg and price was now £45,500.

Against a background of adverse currency rates, falling demand in the vital North American market and speculation as to the continued independence and viability of Jaguar, the 1990 model range benefited from the introduction of the 4.0-litre AJ6-engined XJ6 saloon. Replacing the 3.6, the new engine produced 235 bhp and

5 *From its introduction the Convertible had a more stylish, cohesive look than the more controversial styling of the Coupé and now benefitted further with the neater tail treatment adopted across the range. (J C) 6 Not only did the XJ220 represent a quantum leap forward in terms of supercar performance but it was equipped with unheard of levels of comfort and*

sophistication for such a car. (Philip Porter) 7 Though a large car and immensely fast, the XJ220 was not difficult to drive and was happy to potter through towns or villages, but let it off the leash on roads such as those found in the Yorkshire Dales and it provided one of life's great experiences. (Philip Porter)

8

9

10

The new Insignia range was aimed at further [inten]sfying niche markets and maximising sales [wit]h a so-called bespoke service to offer greater [ind]ividuality to the standard products. (J C) [T]he Jaguar Majestic, which revived a good old [Da]imler name, was approximately five inches [lon]ger to give greater rear seat legroom and [a] raised roof gave increased headroom. (J C) Some seven years after the XJ40 succeeded the [Ser]ies III XJ6, the V12 engine was finally offered [in t]he newer shell, which needed considerable re-[eng]ineering as it was never designed to take the [lar]ger engine. (J C) 11 In May 1993 the XJS [ran]ge was revised once again and benefited from [mo]re stylish and modern moulded bumpers which [we]re a far cry from the ghastly black appendages [of] the early cars. (J C) 12 Although XJS [con]vertibles produced by specialist companies, [suc]h as Lynx, had always had two small rear [sea]ts, Jaguar chose, for various reasons, not to offer [a 2] + 2 Convertible model until 1993. (J C) 13 [Alt]hough pre-empted by the JaguarSport XJR-S, [Jag]uar now chose to fit the enlarged 6.0-litre [ver]sion of the V12 engine in the revised XJS [mo]dels and they gained a considerable [imp]rovement in performance as a result. (J C) 14 [Fo]r the first time in 30 years a new production line [wa]s installed in late 1993 and this allowed the [doo]rs to be removed at the start of the assembly [pro]cess, permitting easier operator access. (J C)

would accept both leaded and unleaded fuel. Catalytic converters were made available as an option for the first time on a Jaguar and the new engine was mated to either a newly developed, electronically controlled, programme switchable 4-speed automatic transmission, or a new generation 5-speed manual gearbox for certain markets. Anti-lock braking was now standard on all models and the interior was revised to incorporate, once again, traditional analogue instruments which replaced the ghastly vacuum fluorescent pack that seemed most inappropriate for a Jaguar.

With its improved low speed torque, this new model was well received and would play an important role in the difficult times ahead. The six-cylinder saloon range now consisted of the XJ6 2.9 at £21,200, the XJ6 4.0 at £25,200, the Sovereign 2.9 at £28,000, the Sovereign 4.0 at £32,500 and the Daimler 4.0 at £36,500. The remaining models available consisted of the Jaguar V12 saloon at £33,500, the Daimler

Double Six saloon at £37,000, the XJS 3.6 Coupé at £27,200, the XJS V12 Coupé at £34,200 and the XJS V12 Convertible at £41,200.

In parallel with the new 4.0 XJ6, JaguarSport announced the XJR 4.0 which had a top speed of 146 mph and, in manual form, could reach 60 mph from standstill in 6.7 seconds. Customers had the option of either a new ZF 4-speed automatic transmission offering *Sport* and *Normal* modes of operation or a manual Getrag 'box.

In late 1989 the press were full of reports concerning predators who wished to take over Jaguar, in spite of the Government's Golden Share which precluded control passing into foreign hands. However, with Jaguar's finances rapidly declining, a lack of investment for future models being generated and suitors in the shape of General Motors and Ford pressing their claims, the Government decided it was prudent to relinquish its Golden Share and the barriers were down. The giants negotiated but when Ford offered

12

14

£1,600m for just £350m of assets and gave a variety of assurances the Jaguar board reluctantly accepted that in reality they had no choice. Therefore Ford took total ownership and thus control of Jaguar, thereby securing its future.

The Ford thinking was that this was a cheaper and faster way of entering the international luxury car market rather than designing and developing a new upmarket range, especially when considering the time it would take to build the necessary image. In Jaguar they had the image but, as they were to find, the investment required was very substantial indeed.

Soon after the Ford takeover, Sir John Egan decided to move on to fresh challenges. Whilst there was still very considerable room for improvement in quality and, due to the currency fluctuations which had so helped his cause when he first took over now being unfavourable, the company was struggling once again, there is no question that he had saved Jaguar in its darkest days. Equally it was going through dark days once more and Bill Hayden was

appointed by Ford to take command and shake up the antiquated plants.

'I've been to car plants all around the world,' he later stated. 'Apart from some Russian factories, Jaguar's was the worst I'd ever seen.' Too late Ford realised it had bought a company with work practices that would have looked out of date in the 1970s. 'He had the ability,' Hayden was quoted as saying of Egan, 'to convince the world that his company had something, when it didn't. It's a rare gift.'

In *Topics*, the magazine for Jaguar employees, he wrote, '1990 has not been an easy year for anyone involved with Jaguar. It has been a period of change, adjustment and uncertainty and will certainly make an interesting chapter in Jaguar's history books. It will be remembered as the beginning of a remarkable new era – an era of growth on a scale never before attempted in the company's long and distinguished history'. The challenge was underlined by the fact that January sales were 51.6% lower than the previous year's.

Meanwhile, the 1990 Motor Show had

seen the debut of the 3.2-litre X which replaced the 2.9 model and, commemorate that year's Le Mans wi some 280 examples of the JaguarSpo Le Mans Special Edition XJS V Coupé were to be produced.

About six months later the XJS can in for radical updating involving ov 1,200 new or modified parts at a investment cost of £50m. In spite nearly 40% of the body panels bein changed the overall appearance wa only marginally altered and th Coupé's controversial rear flyin buttresses were retained. The mo noticeable differences were to be seen the rear end where the treatment wa now softer. The interior was als extensively redesigned and mech anically the most important chang was the adoption of the 4.0-litr engine in place of the 3.6. The V Convertible was now priced at £50,60 In September 1991 JaguarSport intro duced their version of the new V Coupé and in February 1992 it wa announced that from May the XJ Convertible would be available hence

15

16

17

th with the 4.0-litre six-cylinder
gine.

Early in the new year it was revealed
it 1991 total sales at 27,000 had
most halved and were the lowest for
ie years. Losses were variously
ported at £160m, £200m and £260m,
ach of this due to the cost of cutting
200 jobs, a third of the workforce. The
mbined deficit for the three previous
urs was stated to be £350m.

This depressing news was somewhat
set by the undoubted quality of the
w models. Gavin Green, respected
itor of *Car* magazine, wrote
owingly in *The Independent* of the XJ6
had been running for four months
d 8,000 miles. 'It is a lovely car and an
solute bargain compared with the
tentatious Audis, showy Citroëns,
sh Fords, high-falutin Hondas,
etentious Peugeots, ritzy Rovers, self-
portant Saabs, vulgar Vauxhalls or
orst of all) voguish Volvos that cost as
ich and often more, and do a
antifiably inferior job at serving up
kury motoring.'

At the end of March Bill Hayden

retired as Chairman and Chief
Executive after four decades with Ford
of Europe and was succeeded by Nick
Scheele, who had been Vice Chairman
since the beginning of the year. His
predecessor had already made some
fundamental changes to manufacturing,
cutting defect rates to a fifth of what
they had been, improving productivity
by 50% and lowering the company
break-even point by a third. However,
Scheele, a charming and unassuming
man, still had plenty of challenges
ahead. Apart from replacement models
for the existing range, ever since Ford's
takeover there had been talk of a new
Mark II, a smaller car to take on the
5 Series BMW.

A prototype two stroke engine was
unveiled in May which, it was claimed,
could power a new generation of fuel
efficient, low emission, high performance luxury cars. This compact and
light engine was the culmination of a
four and a half year research programme
by a group of engineers at Jaguar's
engine research and development centre
at Whitley, working in conjunction with

the Orbital Engine Corporation of
Australia and Queens University,
Belfast. The prototype 3.6-litre V6 two
stroke engine was 40% lighter than the
V12 power unit yet capable of
producing the same power output.

The quality improvements achieved

*15 The XJ6 Gold, introduced in 1994, was
pitched at the more staid, traditional customer
who might be alarmed by the more overtly racy
Sport models and preferred a softer ride and a
touch more luxury. (J C) 16 The six-door Daimler
Limousine was not produced by the factory being
built by an outside coachbuilding concern. This
was clearly based on the XJ saloons from
Coventry, where the old Daimler Limousines had
ceased production which meant the final demise
of the XK engine (J C). 17 During 1994 the AJ6
engine was re-engineered and fitted first in the
XJS in 4.0-litre form with the aim of creating
more of a sports car to contrast with the Grand
Touring V12-engined version. (J C) 18 Codenamed the X300 during development, the new
XJ saloons announced in late 1994 were, if not a
completely new model, at least very much more
than a mere facelift and represented the first new
model to be introduced since the Ford takeover.
Clockwise from the foreground the XJR,
Daimler Six and XJ12 are shown here. (J C)*

since the Ford acquisition translated into Jaguar offering a three-year, 60,000 mile warranty from June, 1992. Further proof of improving standards was given by the annual US league table of customer satisfaction prepared by J. D. Power and Associates. Jaguar moved up from 25th position in 1991 to 10th in 1992. Sales, though, were still depressed at just 5,434 for the first quarter and translated into a loss of £9,500 on every car sold.

As the search for sales went on, new territories were being explored in the hope of countering a weak home market. A number of joint ventures were set up in such places as Taiwan, and new distributors appointed in Poland and the East of Germany.

In September 1992 the company celebrated its 70th anniversary and announced certain refinements to the range. These included the fitting of a driver's airbag and sophisticated alarm system as standard equipment. The smaller 2.9-litre engined saloons had now been superseded by an enlarged 3.2 version of the AJ6 engine, which also benefited from further noise reduction by the fitting of new camshafts.

Two new initiatives were announced at the 1992 Motor Show, namely the *Insignia* range and the new Majestic models. The *Insignia* name denoted a new, bespoke range of cosmetic options. Customers could in future choose from a selection of ten special exterior colours, together with interiors trimmed in a unique range of matching hides. These were complimented by a choice of natural or tinted wood veneers, and new wheels had been designed with the intention of giving a totally coordinated style. The new Majestic saloons were longer wheelbase versions of the six-cylinder models, and would be available from mid-1993. The 5in (125mm) extra length provided a significant increase in rear seat legroom and headroom was improved by the redesigned roof. Both these new ranges

were to be built by the craftsmen in the Special Vehicle Operations department where the large Daimler limousines had been built for a number of years.

In December 1992 the last Series III model left the production line, concluding a span of 24 years during which over 400,000 examples of the pre-XJ40 range had been completed.

After a hiatus of just two months, the V12 engine reappeared in the XJ40 bodyshell. The new Jaguar XJ12, which was launched at the Amsterdam Show, was fitted with the 6.0-litre version of the 12-cylinder power unit which, though of greater capacity than its predecessor, offered improved economy as well as better performance. Acceleration from standstill to 60 mph was improved from 8.9 seconds, to 6.8 seconds, and top speed was now 155 mph. The even more refined Daimler Double Six was to debut at the Geneva Show in March.

The new year had begun well with improved sales and the XJ6 3.2 won *What Car?* magazine's coveted "Best Luxury Car" award. At the Fleet Motor Show in April, another new model was announced. The XJ6 3.2S was aimed at the younger driving enthusiast who required a tauter handling car, a more sporty exterior and interior, together with a high level of specification for the price. The model could be recognized by its colour coded radiator grille and low profile Pirelli P4000 225/60 ZR 16 tyres.

The fabulous XJ220 supercar was now in small-scale production and the author had been only the second

motoring writer in the world to entrusted with the wheel of an exam Though a very large car, it did not f excessively so. The performance, wit 0–60 time of 8.0 seconds and top spe of 213 mph, felt absolutely sensatio while the limits of the exceptio roadholding could not even be explor on the road. It was an utterly beauti car, brilliantly engineered and super produced. The absolute tragedy was t the gestation period had coincided w a world recession. Not only did the now, sadly, seem inappropriate at t time of economic stringency, but a many of those who had placed th orders struggled to fulfil th commitment. Prices plunged, but one wanted D-types when they were production.

In May Jaguar stole JaguarSpo thunder when they launched a revis XJS range which included a 6.0-li V12 version. The 4.0-litre and 6.0-li Coupé models were fitted with improved sports suspension whi consisted of new Bilstein dampe revisions to the spring rates and fr anti-roll bar specification, deletion the rear anti-roll bar and the fitment low profile tyres. This new suspensi was an optional extra on the Converti models, which were now altered incorporate two small rear sea External alterations included the fitti of new moulded bumpers which ga the ageing XJS a more contempora appearance.

During 1993 the Department Transport published a survey, whi

19 The interior of the new Daimler Double Six, the top of the range model, positively oozed opulence and continued the famous British tradition of fine Connolly leather and the tasteful application of wood veneers. (J C) 20 An exciting innovation for Jaguar was the introduction of a supercharged version of the 4.0-litre engine which gave V12 levels of acceleration and torque, without the heavy fuel consumption. (J C)

19

drawn its data from police reports road accidents involving injury, and ich found that the Jaguar XJ6 range tected its occupants better than any er car in the survey. In claiming that as building the safest car in Britain, uar announced that henceforth a nt passenger side airbag would be a ndard fitment.

ollowing news that Jaguar had nbed one place higher, to ninth ition, in the annual J. D. Power customer satisfaction survey, and ad of BMW, changes were ounced for the 1994 model range. st notably the XJ6 4.0-litre and rereign 3.2-litre saloons were deleted l, following the successful launch of XJ6 3.2S, the XJ6 4.0S was now led to the line-up.

Against a background of rumours that d would allocate production of the ure new smaller saloon, with which it was planned to increase overall production eventually to 100,000 vehicles per year, to a Ford plant at Cologne in Germany and production of the replacement XJS to a factory in the States, a new production line was installed at Browns Lane. The replacement £8.5m assembly line was up and running in just three weeks. The new overhead mounted, doors off, single track assembly line replaced the former twin track saloon car production line which had been installed over thirty years before. Apart from quality and efficiency gains, the new facilities expanded capacity by 25% and provided employees with a much improved working environment.

With sales 36% up in the vital US market, an order from Budget Rent a Car for 500 XJ6 saloons was not only a record for the company but a further welcome boost and proof of confidence in the product. Apart from the obvious benefits of this order which was worth £17m ($25M) at showroom values, it had the side effect of introducing more Americans to the enjoyment of Jaguar motoring and thus the potential to recruit new customers. Back in Britain total car sales rose by 17.8% in August, but Jaguar outperformed the market by recording a jump of 25%. The search for new markets led the company to appoint a distributor for China.

'China is set to become one of our most important development markets,' stated Nick Scheele. 'As with any development market, we will be growing from modest beginnings, but we see tremendous long term potential for Jaguar in China. We expect to sell 40 cars in 1993 rising to over 100 cars next year. This will help to consolidate our strong growth in the Asia Pacific region during the past year.'

In October the company announced the introduction of 10,000 mile or 12 monthly service intervals which, it claimed, was the most comprehensive after-sales customer package in the UK market. It was stated that this initiative would reduce ownership costs for a typical XJ6 owner by some 22% during the period of the standard 3 year/60,000 mile warranty.

Sales for 1993 increased worldwide by 22% from 22,483 to 27,338 cars, with exports accounting for 77% of sales (21,223). While sales in the depressed UK market improved by only 11%, they leapt ahead in the States by a more healthy 47% – from 8,681 to 12,734. Buoyed up by this success, Jaguar launched another model in February 1994. With the XJ6 3.2 reduced in price to £26,950 and the more sporty XJ6 3.2S retailing at £29,950, a new model, the XJ6 Gold, was slotted between the two at £28,950. This new model was aimed at the less sporty, more traditional owner and so the accent was on comfort and luxury. This translated into a little more leather and greater application of veneers, gold badging and twin gold coachlines.

For the second year running Jaguar annexed the "Best Luxury Car" award given by *What Car?* magazine, and Germany's leading car magazine *Auto Motor und Sport* voted the XJ6 range "Top Imported Luxury Car" – ahead of Rolls-Royce, Bentley, Cadillac and Lexus.

With the demise of the old Daimler Limousine, the void was filled by Eagle

Specialist Vehicles, the coachbuilding division of Wilcox & Co (Limousines) Ltd. A six-door version of the standard Daimler saloon was created by stretching the wheelbase some 160 in (4,070 mm). With a raised roofline, it was claimed to provide the most spacious, airy interior of any luxury limousine. An optional row of full size, folding occasional rear seats, increased carrying capacity from five to eight. A hearse version, said to be the largest,

most imposing hearse on the market, was also available!

Following the US order for rental cars, Budget announced in May 1994 that it was ordering 110 cars, the biggest ever single European order for Jaguar, to launch a fleet of Jaguars into the UK and European rental markets. The Department of Transport once again confirmed the XJ saloon as the safest car in Britain, the safety performance being between 45% and 60%

above the average for all cars.

In mid-1994 the XJS range came for further revision. The 4.0-litre eng was comprehensively re-engineered attain improvements in performar durability, refinement, reliability economy. Power was increased to bhp at 4,700 rpm and torque to 282 l at 4,000 rpm. This 4.0-litre model co be distinguished now by its colo keyed grille, door mirrors and headla bezels, whereas the V12 model l

21

rome mirrors and bezels, and a black
lle. The intention was to aim the six-
inder at the younger, sporty
thusiast and the refined, sophisti-
ed 6.0-litre at those rating luxury as a
gher priority.

Late September 1994 saw the
roduction of the completely revised
range of saloons, which had been
de-named X300. Representing an
vestment of £200m, the new XJ series
ffectively the Series V – was the first

major fruition since the Ford takeover
in 1990.

'The new car', stated the company,
'maintains the long heritage of
engineering excellence and styling
pedigree but combines this, for the first
time, with world class manufacturing
process management derived from its
parent company.' The styling was
termed 'retrolutionary', which meant it
was strongly reminiscent of Sir
William's stylish original XJ6 and very
much less bland. Above all, the new cars
had the sculptured bonnet and wings
once more, proving that curves are far
more stylish than flat, or virtually flat,
surfaces. The classic lines were matched
with such modern features as colour-
keyed bumpers, a slimmer radiator
grille and distinctive head and tail light
treatments.

All exposed body panels were made
from double sided, zinc-coated steel and
refinement was enhanced by new door
and body sealing systems. With the
environment in mind, some 40% by
weight of the saloons was to be made
from recycled materials, whilst around
85% by weight would be recyclable.

The AJ6 engine had been so
extensively redesigned that it was
renamed the AJ16. As a result of the
introduction of more than 100 newly
tooled engine and ancilliary components, power, torque and refinement
were significantly improved. Most
exciting of all was the addition of a
supercharged 4.0-litre version. Jaguar's
first ever supercharged luxury saloon
delivered an impressive 326 PS (240
kW) and class leading 378 lb ft (512
Nm) torque at only 3,050 rpm. The 6.0-
litre V12 continued to power the top of
the range models and traction control
was introduced across the range.

That range now consisted of the more

traditional XJ6 3.2, Sovereign 3.2 and
Sovereign 4.0 models; the more sporty,
extrovert XJ Sport 3.2, XJ Sport 4.0 and
supercharged XJR models; and the
prestigious Daimler Six, Jaguar XJ12
and Daimler Double Six models. Prices
began at £28,950 and extended up to
£59,950.

Boosted by the new XJ Series, Jaguar
moved into profit in the last three
months of 1994. Production had risen
by 7% to 31,500 with sales leaping 10%
to 30,000, the US accounting for half
that total. Production of 38,000 was
being predicted for 1995. During 1994
Jaguar agreed to contribute £9.4m to
ensure that production of the X100
project, the exciting, very stylish XJS
replacement, would remain in Britain.
In early 1995 Ford was seeking aid of
between £80m and £100m towards the
£500m planned investment to design
and develop the volume X200 new
smaller car and avoid switching
production to a Ford plant at Wixon,
near Detroit. The press suggested that
the very future of Jaguar as a British-
based company depended on the X200
programme remaining in the UK.
Others suggested that Ford had more
sense than to destroy the unique British
flavour that has always been so much a
part of the character of Jaguar.

One has learnt from a turbulent
couple of decades that only a fool now
makes predictions about Jaguar's future.
In recent times it has risen to the
heights, and sunk to the depths. With
highly professional management, a
slimmed down workforce, the might of
Ford behind the company, somewhat
rejuvenated plants, as fine a product
range as at any time in the company's
long history and, above all, the promise
of three completely new ranges on the
horizon, one is tempted to be optimistic.

*21 The new supercharged XJR gave zest to the
Jaguar range and subtly combined traditional
curvaceous styling with a modern touch, without
being too overtly outlandish. It seems like an ideal
car to power Jaguar into the later nineties. (J C)*

11 JAGUAR COMPETES

Whilst it is clearly impossible to quantify Jaguar's competitive successes in business terms, what is undeniable is that the undoubted technical attributes of their cars came to the public awareness more swiftly and comprehensively than any advertising campaign could have achieved. International success against such august names as Ferrari and Mercedes-Benz demanded international press coverage, and greatly enhanced Britain's name abroad.

1

importance of Jaguar's involvement ompetition and its successes cannot over-stressed. The many internal awards and the resulting glory e done more for the company's ge, and therefore sales, than possibly other single factor. Furthermore, nical development has been aided greatly hastened by racing and rally-Many features first used on com-tion models were later seen on duction cars. Above all, the five Le ns wins in the 1950s ensured that the e of Jaguar would be a legendary one acing history.

fter the war, many of the competi-tion successes were masterminded by another legendary Jaguar figure – Lofty England, who modestly described him-self after the first Le Mans victory in 1951 as 'the sort of unofficial Competi-tion Manager'.

As Lofty said recently, 'We realized that competition was the best way of pro-ducing publicity.' He went on to state that 'winning Le Mans didn't cost us much. I'd be surprised if it cost more than £15,000, but it was most important for it helped our sales in America and this helped our steel quota, which was a problem in the early postwar years.'

In 1976, a journalist writing about the

1 *Outside assistance needed for this SS I Tourer seen tackling a hill during the Barn-staple Trial (*National Motor Museum*) 2 An Austin 7 Swallow Two-Seater receiving assistance on a test hill in Yorkshire, which formed part of the London–Edinburgh trial (J C) 3 Old No 8, the famous SS 100, rounds the top S at Shelsley in September 1937, driven by Sammy Newsome in a best time of 45.52 secs. 4 M. J. Holloway is assisted to the famous start line at Shelsley. Old No 8 had by this time shed its wings and lights. 5 Sammy Newsome has a 'moment' between the esses at the same meeting in May 1938, later recording 43.98 secs (*W. Gibbs, Midland Automobile Club*)*

3

5

D-Type in the American magazine *Road and Track*, did so under the heading of 'The World's Longest-Running Advert'.

In the early days of SS competition activity, the cars won more prizes for styling and concours d'elegance rather than for performance. They initially did little to refute their image of 'more show than go', but gradually notable exceptions caught the motoring public's attention. The open SS Is distinguished themselves on several occasions, and Lyons entered a team of three SS I Tourers in the International Alpine Trial of 1933. Mechnical troubles asserted themselves, but the following year a team award was gained.

The 2½-litre SS100 was the first model to achieve any real distinction in competition circles, and thereby helped to allay the comments about more looks than performance. One of the first successes was the winning of the Glacier Cup and, in effect, overall victory by Tom and Elsie Wisdom in the 1936 International Alpine Trials – an event that was to figure several times in the future.

The car used was owned by the factory and, because of its chassis number – 18008 – came to be known as 'Old No 8'. It was driven in hill-climbs, particularly Shelsley Walsh, by Sammy Newsome (the Coventry garage and theatre owner), and in rallies and races such as Brooklands, by Tom Wisdom.

In 1937 a works team of 2½-litre SS100s was entered in the RAC Rally. The cars were driven by Tom Wisdom, Ernest Rankin (head of publicity), E. H. Jacob, and the Hon Brian Lewis. They won the Manufacturer's Team Prize but first place overall went to the privately entered SS100 of Jack Harrop, with Bob Taylor navigating.

In the Welsh Rally in July, Jacob put up the best overall performance, and the

1 In spite of foul weather, Harrop and Taylor in their privately entered SS 100 beat not only the works team but also all other competitors to finish first in the RAC Rally of 1937 (R. Taylor) 2 Jack Harrop (left), later killed in the war, and Bob Taylor his navigator, prepare for the 1939 RAC Rally, having notched up a second win in 1938 (R. Taylor) 3 Harrop and Taylor hurling the SS 100 through the driving test stage of the 1939 RAC Rally (R. Taylor) 4 In spite of victories in 1937 and 1938, the best Harrop and Taylor could manage in 1939 was eighth (R. Taylor) 5 An SS 100 leaves the Great West Road starting point with 500 miles ahead through the Welsh countryside

team again took the Manufacturer's Prize. In October they won a 'long handicap' at Brooklands with Old No 8 now fitted with an experimental $3\frac{1}{2}$-litre engine.

After their fine drive in the 1937 RAC Rally, Lyons invited Harrop and Taylor to join the works team for the 1938 event. It proved to be a good move because they brought the $3\frac{1}{2}$-litre 100 to a win in the class for open cars over 15 hp. The same class was won by Mrs V. E. M. Hetherington in the Welsh Rally in her SS100, and Tom Wisdom added a first in class

on the Paris–Nice Trial to his list of successes.

At an SS Car Club meeting at Donington, Lyons himself won a race for 'trade drivers', from Newsome and Bill Heynes, all in SS100s, of course.

Tom Wisdom writing some years later, stated 'As catalogued, the $3\frac{1}{2}$-litre engine developed 125 bhp on a compression ratio of 7 to 1. What was its ultimate limit, modified for racing? Hassan and designer Heynes decided to find out. Encouraged by the robust bottom end they experimented with magneto igni-

tion and a compression like a seizure, to 1 to be exact. This called for metha fuels.'

Old No 8, fitted with this $3\frac{1}{2}$-l engine, continued to gain successes Shelsley and elsewhere, and the eng was further developed until it was giv at least 160 bhp which, interestingly, the target set for the XK engine.

Apart from the engine, the body chassis also came in for attention. body gradually shed parts such as wii and lights. It was given a neat, round tail, and the chassis was extensively d

1

2

3

for lightness.

he 1939 rally season opened with the ous Monte Carlo event and Jack rop, this time without Bob Taylor, had business commitments, shed in tenth equal place, driving an Jaguar 3½-litre saloon. The RAC ly resulted in a second in class for wsome (not in Old No 8) and second he club Team Prize. In June, New-e gave Old No 8 its final prewar run Shelsley, and a win in the 3001-o cc unsupercharged class was his ard. Finally, in July W. C. N.

Norton won his class, and Miss V. Watson took the Ladies' Prize (open cars) in the Welsh Rally.

SS100s continued to be used to great effect after the war and some of the model's greatest successes were gained in the early postwar years. With a dearth of race meetings, 100s distinguished themselves at sprints and hill-climbs, such as Prescott, Naish House and Shelsley. Ian Appleyard finished third in the 1947 Alpine Trial in his nine-year-old car. A year later he was back with a 'new' car – LNW 100, this being a car

1 *Bertie Bradnack waiting to commence a run at Shelsey Walsh (B. Bradnack)* 2 *W. H. Waring and W. H. Wadham take their 3½-litre Mark V through the braking and acceleration tests to finish ninth in the 1951 Monte – they were placed second in the Coachwork 'Comfort' Contest afterwards (Fox)* 3 *Leslie Johnson wrestles manfully and effectively with the XK 120 in its first race at Silverstone in 1949* 4 *Following Bira's spin Johnson took over the lead and Walker (seen here) finished second in the Production Car Race* 5 *Johnson crosses the finishing line to give the XK 120 its maiden victory first time out (J C)*

stored throughout the war and first registered in 1947. With this famous car he won a coveted Coupe des Alpes, and finished first in class. In 1949 Appleyard finished second in the Tulip Rally with the same car.

Various other examples continued to be rallied in the early 1950s with some success, but gradually other makes and, in particular, the XK120s, took over.

In spite of the Jabbeke demonstration of the XK120, a show of the XK's racing prowess was needed. An opportunity presented itself when the BRDC announced that they would be holding a production car race at their August 1949 meeting. Before committing himself, Lyons wanted to be sure that the Jaguars could win, so a standard 120 was taken down to Silverstone.

Lofty England takes up the story. 'We had to prove the car would go round corners, as well as go quickly in a straight line. Sir William said we would compete if an example could be driven for three hours non-stop under the lap record without breaking down. We hadn't got any racing drivers, only a couple of chaps called England and Hassan. So we did the driving. I tried to go quickly and Hassan tried to break it. Being in the experimental department, it was his job to break things. He always believes there is something wrong if he can't break it!'

Gradually they increased their speed, approaching and eventually breaking the lap record. Walter Hassan remembers the occasion well. In trying to go faster, he 'went through the bales several times and ended up with a bashed bonnet with straw all over it!' He also remembers that 'Bill Lyons said that he must try it for himself, called Rankin to join him and set off.' As they approached the first corner Lyons turned to his passenger and said 'Rankin, I've left my specs behind, indicate which way to go and thump me on the back when I must brake'. When they returned to the pits, Lyons noticed the look of fright on Rankin's face and 'laughed like hell'.

'It was decided that Hassan could prepare the cars,' recalled Lofty, 'and some old boy called England could be pit manager or something.'

For the race, Jaguar did not officially enter, but lent three cars – painted individually red, white and blue – to Leslie Johnson, Prince Bira (the blue one of course) and Peter Walker. Bira was leading when, as a result of a puncture (the wing strut was fouling the tyre wall) he spun and could not regain the course. However, Johnson won at an average speed of 82.8 mph and Peter Walker was a good second.

Six aluminium cars were sold or lent to six selected drivers in 1950. They were works cars in all but name. Leslie Johnson had JWK 651 and it was arguably the most active of all, finishing fifth in the Mille Miglia of that year. This car along with two others was entered in the 1950 Le Mans 24-hour race merely as an experiment, because it was not expected to win, but much would be learnt about its potential, etc., that might be applied in the future. The car ran well and was in third place after 21 hours and gaining

on the leaders when unfortunately t clutch succumbed. The car was retire but valuable lessons had been learnt.

In October 1950 Johnson, with Mc sharing the driving, completed a 24 hour endurance test at the Montlhe track near Paris. The car covered the la hour at an average speed of 112.40 mp

An important date for Jaguar and an up-and-coming young driver call Stirling Moss, was 16th Septemb because it was the date of the Tou Trophy, at Dundrod, Ulster. To

1

2

134

sdom, who owned JWK 688, another
he six works cars, had recognized the
ing driver's inherent skill and offered
end him his XK120 for the race. Moss
s quick to accept because he was keen
get some sports racing experience.
uar, however, were none too pleased
earn that an inexperienced youngster
uld be handling one of their works
s. From the drop of the flag, Johnson
JWK 651 led, but Moss quickly
ght and passed him. Just before the
rt, the skies had opened and the track

was hit by a sustained deluge. Many
spun off and crashed, and it was said that
the wind was blowing so strongly that it
was almost a physical impossibility to
steer a straight course. Rain was not
unusual in this area and there was a local
saying, 'If you can see the hills, it's going
to rain; if you can't see the hills, it
already is.'

After two hours racing, Moss was two
minutes ahead of Whitehead in another
XK120 who was, in turn, 27 seconds
ahead of Johnson. Next came Parnell,

1 *A MK V, having started from Glasgow,
descends Hucks Brow on the Shap Fell en route
for Monte Carlo in 1951 (Fox)* **2** *The Flying
Mantuan, Tazio Nuvolari, practised for the
1950 Silverstone event but sadly was too ill for
the race (National Motor Museum)* **3** *The
Moss/Johnson car high on the Monthlery banking during their 100 mph plus run for 24 hours
(National Motor Museum)* **4** *The
Whitehead/Marshall car at speed at the 1950
Le Mans finished 15th after a steady run (J C)*
5 *Young Stirling Moss takes the chequered flag
after his quite amazing drive in the 1950 TT
that earned him a works drive (J C)*

5

Abecassis and Macklin in relative comfort in their DB2 saloons. Shortly afterwards, the press tent blew down and the pits were constantly threatened with flooding.

After two-and-a-half hours, Moss had averaged 76.02 mph, about 98% of his target, and had been given the 'Slow' signal by his father. But, very near the end Alfred Moss, whose race records had been ruined by the weather, heard a rumour that Bob Gerard in a Frazer Nash, who had been driving through the field, had pulled up so much on handicap that he was now ahead of Stirling. So,

with just one lap to go, Stirling's father hung out the 'Flat Out' sign and his son calmly responded in the increasing gloom by putting in a last lap at 77.61 mph, a Dundrod TT record.

The day after the race was Moss's 21st birthday, and as a result of this drive, Lyons invited him to drive officially for the factory the following year. When I asked him recently how he viewed the chance Wisdom gave him, Moss replied, 'Oh, that was my first big, big opportunity in motor racing because I had asked a lot of people at that time if they would let me drive their cars in the TT, which

was one of the classic races of the peri[od] but none of them would trust me. Th[ey] thought I was going too fast for [my] experience, and if I was going to have [an] accident and kill myself they didn't wa[nt] me to do it in their car, so none of t[he] companies, including MG and all [the] much lesser companies, would let [me] have one, and I was very grateful [to] Tommy Wisdom to fix up so that I co[uld] borrow his.'

Perhaps the most famous and succe[ss]ful combination of car and driver ever [to] be seen in the world of rallying was [Ian] Appleyard and his XK120 Super Spo[rts]

1

2

istered and known simply as
JB 120.

Appleyard, as described earlier, had
ady tasted success with his SS100 –
IW 100 – and was something of an
pine specialist. This rally in 1950 was
be his first with his new mount. He
up a fine performance and a penalty-
e run, the fastest speed over the flying
ometre; and fastest time on the Col de
rs hill climb resulted in a class win and
restigious Coupe des Alpes. This suc-
s prompted *The Motor* in its editorial
state, 'The great Jaguar Alpine per-
mance this year raises Britain's

engineering prestige in many lands.'

A first position overall followed in the
Tulip Rally early in 1951, and to this
were added more minor successes such
as victory in the Morecambe Rally, and
more importantly, another first in the
RAC Rally of that year. The Alpine
Rally provided a second Coupe des
Alpes for another penalty-free run with
his car, and entry in the London Rally
ended in another best performance.

The 1951 Production Car Race at the
Silverstone International Trophy Meeting showed just how popular 120s were
for circuit racing. The result was a fore-

1 *Ian and Pat Appleyard and their famous
XK120, NUB 120, proved virtually unbeatable in the rally world of the early 1950s* (Fox)
2 *Silverstone, 1951, the Production Car Race.
As one might have expected, Moss walked away
from the field beating the likes of Dodson,
Hamilton, Wicken, Johnson and Wisdom, all
in Jaguars* (J C) **3** *In 1951, Moss and factory
man Frank Rainbow took this XK on the Mille
Miglia but crashed out* (J C) **4** *C. Mann competing in the Eastbourne Rally in his early steel-
bodied 120 Roadster* (National Motor
Museum) **5** *Frank Grounds competing in the
Morcambe Rally loses a rear spat – a not
uncommon occurrence* (D. Grounds)

5

going conclusion. Moss finished first followed by Dodson, Hamilton, Wicken and Johnson in XKs, a DB2 finished next, followed by Holt and Wisdom in more XKs – seven of the first eight places – dominance indeed.

In 1952 Appleyard and NUB 120 completed their hat-trick in the Alpine Rally, gaining another penalty-free run. This meant another Coupe des Alpes, the third consecutive Coupe, which achievement won for the Jaguar distributor whose navigator Pat was Sir William's daughter, the first Alpine Gold Cup ever to be awarded.

Apart from NUB 120, XK120s were rallied far and wide. The French International Rallye du Soliel in 1951 was an XK benefit, with examples finishing in first, second, third, fourth and sixth places. That same year, Wood won the Scottish Rally in his 120. Later in the year, Johnny Claes and Jacques Ickx (father of the Grand Prix driver) won the notoriously tough Liège–Rome–Liège Rally in HKV 455, covering the 3,000-mile course without a single mark lo[st] which at the time was a uniq[ue] achievement.

Domestic successes abounded, w[ith] wins in the Welsh Rally, the MCC Ra[lly,] the Rally Automobile Yorkshire a[nd] many others.

In terms of XK competition histo[ry,] the big achievement of 1952 was gain[ed] by the fixed-head, LWK707. This c[ar,] the second to be produced, had be[en] used by Bill Heynes for everyday tran[s]port. It was taken to the French circ[uit]

1

2

3

Montlhery in August and driven by
nson, Fairman, Hadley and Moss for
en days and seven nights, covering
851 miles in 168 hours at an average
ed of more than 100 mph. Such was
acclaim, that the car and drivers were
en a civic reception by the Mayor of
ver on their return. The car was
ven back to London by Laurence
neroy, Technical Editor of *The
tor*, who found everything to be in
fect order, the car betraying no signs
he marathon it has just completed.

Stirling Moss, reminded by me
recently of the run recalled, 'It (the
track) was very rough, but it was interesting because it was quite an achievement for that car to actually do that
length of run. I must say from my point
of view it was very tiring because of the
monotony – no, not tiring so much as
boring, because you just went round and
round, and I remember one time coming
round, I saw what I thought was a pretty
girl. And I called in on our intercom
thing, because we had a radio on it, and

1 *The third XK120 FHC to be produced had,
like many XKs, a competition career*
(National Motor Museum) **2** *The XK120
FHC crossed the line at Monthlery having
covered 16,851 miles in 168 hours at more than
100 mph. Capitalizing on the achievement, the
7 days and 7 nights car is shown to the public
at Earls Court in 1952* (Fox) **3** *Johnson used
his old faithful aluminium-bodied 120 on the
1952 RAC Rally and would have finished third
but was penalized for running without the spats*
(Fox)

I said "What's that bird like?", and they said to me, "she's terrific," so every time I went past I blew her a kiss. Unfortunately, when I stopped at the end, she turned out to be a bit of a dog, so it was all an anti-climax, but they pulled my leg on it terribly!'

The Mark VII saloons showed on innumerable occasions that, in spite of their size and weight, they came from a genuinely sporting background by winning a great many Touring Car races over a period of several years, and also by achieving good placings in various rallies.

In 1953, Ian Appleyard forsook XKs, which were no longer eligible for the Monte Carlo Rally, for a Mark VII and finished a fine second in the general classification. In his new XK, registered RUB 120, Appleyard won another Coupe des Alpes. At the International Trophy at Silverstone, the same year, Moss drove a Mark VII to victory in the Touring Car race, and at the same me ing the following year it was Appleyar turn to lead home Rolt and Moss, all Mark VIIs. The same year Ron Adams and Desmond Titterington their Mark VII proved to be the high placed British entry in the Monte Ca Rally with a sixth place. Another exa ple of the model, driven by Cecil Va came eighth.

Following the distinguished showi of the virtually standard XK120s in t

1

2

3

o Le Mans race Lyons eventually
e the go-ahead to design a serious
llenger for outright honours in 1951.
was fired perhaps by the atmosphere
he event that Jaguar's had found to
r surprise they had a good chance of
ning or, more likely, he was confi-
t that a specially designed Jaguar
rts racing car could succeed where a
duction car had only just failed.
ut in spite of that permission having
n given, during the same busy year,
work on the new car could not begin
until October of that year because the
more important tasks of getting into full
production the new Mark VII and the
steel-bodied 120s, which had by this
time replaced the earlier aluminium
cars, had to take precedence.

Bearing in mind the lessons learned
from 1950, and the fact that all major
components had stood up well, the C-
Type was to have much in common with
the 120, but attention was turned to

lightness, aerodynamics, braking and
handling. The chassis consisted of a fully
triangulated frame of round tubing of
varying diameters. This frame was further stiffened by front and rear bulk-
heads of steel sheet welded to the frame
to aid torsional rigidity. This lightweight
frame was clothed with a good-looking
aerodynamic aluminium shell.

The new car used the XK engine basically unchanged but with some important modifications. Larger exhaust valves
($1\frac{5}{8}$) were fitted and the exhaust porting
was enlarged. Valve lift was increased by
a newly designed camshaft and twin 2-in
SUs were fitted to the majority of C-
Types. In this form the engine gave just
over 200 bhp.

The C-Type front suspension was
closely related to that of the 120, with
wide-based wishbones, longitudinal torsion bars and telescopic hydraulic
dampers. Steering was greatly improved
by the adoption of a rack-and-pinion set-
up. But the rear suspension was completely new. It consisted of a Salisbury
axle and a single transverse torsion bar.
These were attached by a pair of radius
arms further supplemented by an A
bracket designed not only to provide
lateral location of the axle but also to har-
ness the torque reaction provided by
fierce acceleration and use it to reduce
the right hand rear wheel's habit of lift-
ing and spinning.

Braking was improved by the adoption of a new Lockheed self-adjusting
hydraulic two-leading shoe system. This
was kept cool by the use of 16-inch wire
wheels.

Finished just six weeks before the
race, three C-Types were entered for Le
Mans in 1951, driven by Moss/Fairman,
Walker/Whitehead and Johnson/
Biondetti. Lofty England remembers an
amusing incident in practice. 'During
practice Peter Walker, a very good driver
indeed, came in complaining he couldn't
go any faster. He had some strange tinted
goggles on and I told him to put some
clear ones on and he went out and broke
the lap record!'

In the race Moss, who had been paired
with Jack Fairman because of the latter's
Le Mans experience, set a cracking pace

1 *A still hirsute Stirling Moss drove in the*
works' C-Type team at Le Mans in 1951 (J C)
2 *A wooden model of the C-Type used for wind-*
tunnel testing (J C) 3 *A stage in the arrival*
at the final C-Type shape (J C) 4 *The sorry*
state of PDH 33 after black ice led to an excur-
sion and a meeting with what must have been
a very solid tree (B. Bradnack) 5 *Drivers*
Walker (right) and Whitehead show the relief
and satisfaction of victory in the 1951 Le Mans
event (J C)

and gave the continentals a taste of things to come by repeatedly breaking the lap record with ease. But a possible 1, 2, 3 was ruined when Biondetti retired with a broken oilpipe flange. When Moss was put out with the same trouble, the Jaguar pit began to worry that the same problem might afflict the leading Whitehead and Walker car. Meanwhile, the opposition in the shape of $4\frac{1}{2}$-litre Talbots, Ferraris, and 5.4-litre Cunninghams fell by the wayside, most of

them defeated by Moss's early pace. So eventually Whitehead and Walker were able to cruise home victors by 67 miles. Lofty England describes the closing stages. 'Towards the end of the race the Walker/Whitehead car had built up a threequarter-of-an-hour lead which I felt was quite sufficient, and put out the SLOW sign so as to conserve the car. However, Sir William had been persuaded by somebody else that this was not sufficient and he told me to put out the

FASTER sign. I did so, but in a way t Walker couldn't see it. Quite obviou he continued at the same pace and William noticed this and said, "Sure can see it, England? Better stick it a bit further." We then had a situat whereby I was showing the FAST signal when Sir William was looking the SLOW one when he wasn't. P Walker got rather confused, so I ha word with Whitehead who was due take over shortly. I gave him a stopwa

told him to time himself, keep to a ―ain time and *ignore all signals*. We ―g out FASTER signs regularly, but ―ir William commented, "Not mak― ―much difference England"!'

―Videspread acclaim and generous ―licity were the rewards for a famous ―ory, and the year was completed with ―cond win for young Moss in the TT, ―ing a C-Type.

―or the 1952 Mille Miglia a single C-―e was entered for Stirling Moss and

Jaguar chief test driver Norman Dewis, and it was a most significant event for the

1 *Moss takes his second TT, driving the works C-Type that bears his favourite number (J C)* **2** *The development disc-braked C-Type driven in the Mille Miglia by Stirling Moss (N. Dewis)* **3** *The fateful long-nose C-Type that was to fail so miserably at Le Mans in 1952 (J C)* **4** *Duncan Hamilton, who raced Cs far and wide, negotiates the famous Goodwood chicane (J C)* **5** *William Heynes makes notes at*

two. Firstly, the car was fitted with disc brakes, which had been jointly

Jabbeke where, in April 1953, a Mark VIII, XK120 and C-Type were run, achieving 121, 141 and 148 mph, respectively (J C) **6** *The 1953 C-Types, now equipped with Webers and disc brakes, pull up outside the Restaurant des Hunundières on the Mulsanne Straight, showing that they were driven to events. The spare car is the other 17 on the right (National Motor Museum)*

6

developed by Jaguar and Dunlop, and secondly, stories brought home of the Mercedes' straight-line speed were to have dire effects in the near future. This event was nothing more than an experiment for Jaguar and, although lying third at one point, the car retired.

Norman, who had joined the factory as chief test driver in 1952, described to me recently the background to the disc brake development. 'When I first joined, the big push was for disc brakes, and that was my first project. I knew the people at Dunlop and we had a good tie-up. There was a good team build-up between Jaguars and Dunlop, and Mr Heynes said to me "You've got the car, get on with the development", and the first trial disc brake was put on the XK120 by Dunlop. In those days it wasn't the great big empire it is today, and there were probably only about five people involved. It was just a matter of test, test, test, until we got it right. There were problems right at the start. Nobody had any idea of what temperature the discs would run at, or the pad material, because adapting it from an aircraft brake to a car brake was an entirely different thing. You see, on the aircraft they had what we called the "wheel slide protector", where you can't lock a wheel. Well we looked at that, but it was OK on an aircraft because you'd got plenty of space. A pilot just pushed a lever on and that was it, you had maximum "decel" without locking, and of course they only do one stop and then taxi in. So really it was an entirely different requirement for the car, and temperatures were our problem for a start.

'The unit was inside the wheel and we hadn't realized what sort of airflow or air-ducting we needed to cool it, so all this was trial and error. We were seeing temperatures after a few laps of 500° and 600°C. I could finish up with the disc glowing dull red and the fluid almost bursting into flame, but it was only that way we found out and we realized we had to do something about cooling. So first we fitted wire wheels to get air from the outside, and then we had ducts in the front to bring air in on the inside of the brake, and gradually we got the temperatures down to a sensible level. We did most of our testing at Purden, a disused aerodrome just outside Wolverhampton, which Dunlop hired from the Air Ministry.

We used to go there every day, seven days a week. It was nothing to knock up five or six hundred miles a day. We used to be there at half-past-eight in the morning and stay there until it was dark

at seven o'clock in the evening. We did thousands of miles that way, but it was the only way that we got it done quickly. We were ready to go to the Mille Miglia in 1952 with a brake which we knew very little about. But we thought it was the right sort of race, with the distance to be covered, so that we could see (a) just how the brake did perform and (b) what the pad life would be.

'Stirling Moss, for whom I co-drove, was briefed on the situation that we hadn't raced it before, although he knew all the work we'd done, and of course he was very interested in it, because to have

something that your competitors have got is worth quite a lot in a ra Fortunately, we didn't strike any gr problems with the brake. It was certai a very great feature when we were rac against Caracciola in the Merc. caught up with him and, I don't kn how long we were with him, it was di cult to say, but probably about 60 or miles, and we were able to outbrake h every time. He couldn't understand i all. We could see him look every time was "decelling" like mad, and under braking we went by still flat out, and th put the brakes on in front of him. He s

as incredible. Several times he didn't
[th]ink the car was going to stop.'

[M]oss on another occasion recalling
[the] same event, stated, 'Yes, actually the
[disc] brakes in their early days were prone
[to a]ll sorts of problems, knock-off, and
[vap]orization, and goodness knows what
[els]e, and we learnt an awful lot with the
[Jag]uar, with the C-Type particularly,
[abo]ut disc brakes. The trouble with
[the]m was that they were really powerful,
[but] then when you used them once you
[cou]ldn't use them again for quite a while
[unt]il they'd cooled off, because of the
[vap]orization of the fluid, and then you

got knock-off and so on. So, because
Jaguar were racing at the time, because
Dunlop and Girling agreed to work
together with Jaguar, that I think is the
reason disc brakes came about as fast as
they did.'

Le Mans 1952 is best forgotten
because in Jaguar terms it was a complete disaster. The stories about the
Mercedes' superiority panicked the factory into producing a more streamlined
body for the C just weeks before the race.
A hastily designed new cooling system
to suit the lower bodywork was a complete failure and all three cars retired

early on with dire-overheating.

In this period Stirling Moss
attempted to persuade Lyons to build a

1 *Moss (driving) and Peter Walker took this
car to second place at Le Mans in 1953 behind
their team mates, after they had been delayed
early on (*National Motor Museum*) 2 Victory, exhaustion and elation on the faces of (left
to right) Angela Hamilton, Duncan Hamilton,
Tony Rolt, Lois Rolt, mechanic Len Hayden
and Norman Dewis (*N. Dewis*) 3 Le Mans
victors Hamilton and Rolt do a lap of honour
at the British GP at Silverstone in July 1953
(*J C*)*

Grand Prix engine. At that time the cars eligible for the World Championship were Formula 2 two-litre machines. The old XK100 four-cylinder engine was brought out of mothballs, and one example was prepared but sadly never used again.

C-Types had a fair mixture of success in 1952 and 1953 in private hands and with official entries. That this success was not more overwhelming can largely be attributed to the fact that the car was designed to win Le Mans, which was basically all that the factory seriously attempted to do.

One event at Goodwood in 1952 sticks in England's mind. 'Hamilton was leading comfortably with just a few laps to go, when suddenly he was missing. We heard he had gone off somewhere and expected to see him pottering along with a bent car. But he didn't appear. Then there was a commotion behind us and Hamilton appeared carrying a wheel, complete with drum and hub assembly. He chucked it down and announced disgustedly, "There, that's cost me 50 bottles of gin." Duncan in those days calculated everything in bottles of gin!'

For Le Mans 1953, the bodywork was back to 1951 configuration, but Weber carburettors, a lighter chassis and body, beefed-up rear suspension and, of course, disc brakes, distinguished these cars from the earlier ones mechanically. This last-named feature was by far the most important because it allowed Jaguars to set a killing pace while the Ferraris, Alfa Romeos, Cunninghams and Aston Martins had brake fade to contend with. The Cs could stop repeatedly from 140 mph plus in a shorter distance and without a trace of fade. Putting it simply, these disc brakes won the 1953 Le Mans for Jaguar and C-Types finished in first, second and fourth places.

The winning C was driven by Tony Rolt and Duncan Hamilton. Rolt, arguably one of the finest drivers Britain has ever produced, commenced his marathon experience by competing before the war in the 24-hour Grand Prix at Spa Francorchamps while he was still at Eton – indeed, he had to be driven to the event because he was too young to hold a British driving licence. Following a distinguished war career, in which he won the Military Cross and Bar for the defence of Calais and his escaping activities, including Colditz, he formed his famous partnership with Hamilton for Le Mans 1950 and 1951 in Nash Healeys, finishing fourth and sixth respectively.

After continually pestering Lofty England, Rolt was taken to Dundrod in

1951 as a reserve driver, taking over during the race the C of the unwell Johnson. He proceeded to break the lap record a number of times and worked the car up from seventh to fourth. This performance was sufficient to earn him a regular works drive for 1952. Following their earlier success together it seemed obvious that Hamilton should join Rolt in the Jaguar team for all long-distance events.

One of the last great characters of motor racing, 'Ham' drove hard and played hard. For him it was sport for sport's sake, money just did not enter into it. The Rolt/Hamilton success at Le Mans 1953 was all the more remarkable

because the event featured perhaps strongest entry ever seen, with aln every European manufacturer repres ted and most Grand Prix dri competing.

Not surprisingly, this victory att ted much praise and attention. *The D. Telegraph* described it as 'Brita greatest motor-race triumph of all ti and Mintex headed their advertisem 'Salute to a fitting and glorious vic in Britain's Coronation Year!' *Autos* paid tribute with a special green co and their editorial stated that this vic 'had gained the admiration of the wl world . . . no praise can be high eno for all concerned'.

1

2

During 1953 Jaguar produced a proto- [type] that has come to be known in [pr]ospect as the C/D. At the time [Ma]lcolm Sayer referred to it as the [XK]120C Mark II and it has also been [call]ed the Prototype D-Type, and the [ligh]t alloy chassis XPII; and *Autosport* [men]tioned a photograph of the car as [a Co]ventry Disco: a prototype "Disco [Vol]ante" Jaguar, one of several new [typ]es built by the Coventry concern for [spo]rts car races.' Because the last C- [Typ]e was numbered XKC053, this car [was] designated XKC054. It was quite [lite]rally a stepping stone from the C- [Typ]e to the D-Type that was to be. It was [of] alloy monocoque construction but

did not have such good aerodynamic properties as the D. It suffered from having a greater frontal area, presumably because it embodied the wet-sump C-Type engine.

The C/D made only two semi-public appearances. One was at Jabbeke, where Norman Dewis took an XK120, fitted with undershield and bubble top, and proceeded to achieve the quite remarkable speed of 172.412 mph.

The C/D that achieved 178.383 mph was therefore not so impressive although it may have had a problem with the fuel system because the car was not pulling well at the top end. Norman Dewis told me recently that 'in comparison

with the XK it was struggling at the beginning of the measured mile.'

The second and last appearance of the car was at a test prior to the '54 Le Mans, where the factory also had the

1 *The results of the C/D's Jabbeke runs, officially tabulated (J C)* 2 *Hamilton tries the C/D at Silverstone (N. Dewis)* 3 *Dewis at speed with the many-named prototype, which was so reminiscent of the later E-Type and a certain mid-engined car (N. Dewis)* 4 *The entire Jabbeke entourage surrounds the specially prepared XK120. Malcolm Sayer, wearing the jacket, leaning on the XK's bonnet (N. Dewis)*

prototype D. The C/D was immediately overshadowed by the D, with its better aerodynamic qualities and, as a result, development was concentrated on the latter.

Although the C/D was forgotten and eventually broken up, it was not without significance in the evolution of the Jaguar sports racing car. What is particularly interesting is that from most angles it looked rather like the E-Type of eight years later.

As previously mentioned, Norman Dewis took an XK120 'to get some publicity before the Motor Show', according to England, to the familiar ground of the Jabbeke motorway. There were aerodynamic improvements but relatively little mechanical modification. 'Don't go too fast, Norman,' instructed Lofty. 'Take it a bit steady first time'. Dewis takes up the story. 'We thought we would probably see 161/162, which would have been ample, and Malcolm Sayer said he wouldn't like to visualize it going any quicker, because it would just go airborne, and I still don't know how it stayed on the road now! I think fortunately for me, there was not a breath of wind. I am afraid if there had been possibly a gust blowing on the car at threequarters angle, I think it might have started pushing it off. The rev limit I was told from the work they had done on the test bed was five-five/five-six – that should be alright. Well, I had already got up to six before I got to the measured mile, you see, so I thought, well, I can't back off now, I must keep this going. It was beautiful, there was no problem, so I just held it there and got six-two all the way through.

'It did wander a bit. It was a dual carriageway but although you've got two lanes, it doesn't look very wide at that speed. It did weave a bit but I think that was because it was going a bit light on the front end and the rear was probably steering it a bit, that was all. We only had one problem. It was a good job I did a trial run on the day before. We had a cockpit bubble which was screwed down on top of me, and I went straight down Jabbeke just trying it. I'd got around 80/90, then 100, 120, 130, 140, and there was traffic on the road, and I was so engrossed looking at the instruments, the rev counter, the oil temperature, water and all that, that I'd gone a bit farther than I had anticipated, at least 12 or 13 miles. I then cut across the grass centre and went down the other side, and it was halfway down the other side, I started to feel a bit hazy, and I suddenly realized I'd got no air coming in at all, just heat and fumes. I thought, God, I

can't open this canopy, I felt I'd got to open it, but I thought, if I push my fist through it that's going to ruin it, so I just gulped as much air as I could and held my breath and got back. I was virtually collapsing and when they opened it they said I looked like a red tomato! We remedied it by cutting some small louvres in the canopy, but it was just as well we had the trial run and found out, otherwise it might have spoilt the proper runs.'

At the completion of the runs England phoned Lyons who immediately asked,

'How did you get on?' 'Not very v sir,' replied England, '172'. 'Yes, but what's that in mph?'

To keep the competition chaps their toes, Lyons would occasion produce a mock-up of his own in c junction with Fred Gardner who superintendent of the sawmill. One s animal was the Brontosaurus, as it nicknamed, a veritable monster.

Dewis recalls, 'Gardner would ne let anyone in his shop no matter who were, and we knew something was go on because Sir William was popp

1

2

wn there in the evenings about five
ock and staying till around nine.
en we heard they were building a car
all sorts of rumours were going
nd that it was going to be a new sports
with a small engine'. The experimen-
shop then made it into a runner and
wis was asked to test it. On asking Sir
lliam what it was intended for, he
eived the reply, 'It's not for racing
it might offer something for record-
aking'. However, it was only ever run
o or three times at Gaydon on their
two-mile runway'.

Around this time Jaguar thoughts
again turned to Grand Prix racing. For
1954 the engine limit was to be 2½ litres,
and a 2.4 version of the XK engine was
developed with this in mind. Furthermore, two or more C-types were
cannibalized to build a single-seater.
Basically, two C frames were cut in half
and the front halves welded back to
back. Various all-enveloping single-seat
bodies were drawn and one mock-up
built, but the project proceeded no further because the sports cars were gaining
all the publicity required.

The XK140 did not enjoy the same
dramatic competition success as the
XK120 for several reasons. Competitors
had by now had some time to catch up
and both racing and rallying were begin-

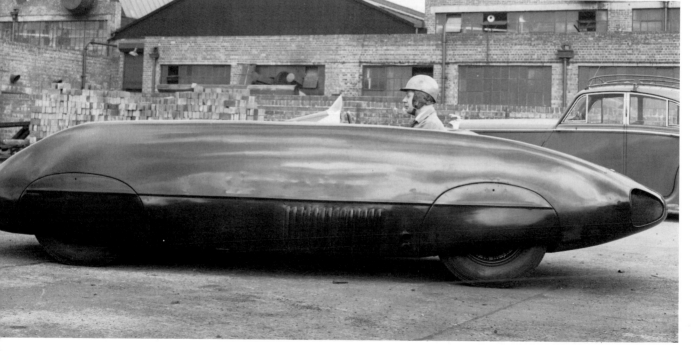

ning to develop into the more professional science that they have become today. The factory, though never officially, prepared XK120s for selected entrants; but to the best of my knowledge, they never prepared any 140s to any great extent. They had intended to have a trio of rally-prepared 140 Roadsters but, sadly, the uncertainty surrounding the future of a number of international events following the Le Mans disaster caused the abandonment of these plans.

But a number of private enthusiasts entered XK140s in diverse events around the world with a fair share of success. One such competitor was none other than Ian Appleyard who had replaced his second 120 Roadster with VUB 140, a special equipment 140 FHC. Although officially retired, he entered a few domestic events with the car, and in 1956 came second overall in the RAC Rally, which was no mean feat. In the same year, Guyot won his class in a 140 Roadster in the Mille Miglia.

In fact, 120s continued to clock up successes in a variety of events. In May 1954, Gillie Tyrer presumably in a Fixed Head, finished second in a Closed Car Race at Ibsley. In July, Haddon and Vivian continued the model's success in the International Alpine Rally with a win. The same month Lord Louth took his class at the Bouley Bay hillclimb in Jersey, and a month earlier Mike Salmon had similar success in the Bo'ness Speed Trials. In August Bob Berry finished third behind Michael Head (father of present Williams Grand Prix designer Patrick Head) in a C-Type at Snetterton, and came second in the O'Boyle Trophy Handicap Race at The Curragh. And still in August, a trio of 120s occupied the first three places in a production car race in Ohio.

The legendary D-Type, successor to the C-Type and evolved from the C/D prototype, was first seen at the private Le Mans test session early in 1954. In just three laps (two more than the officials had given permission for) Rolt proceeded to break the previous year's lap record, set up by Ascari's Ferrari, by five seconds. Such was a foretaste of things to come, of a racing career that was to last more than six years and would include innumerable wins all over the world including three at Le Mans – the race the car was designed to win.

Jaguar and Sir William, as has already been stated, knew the immense publicity value to be gained from success at Les Vingt-Quatre Heures du Mans, which considerably outweighed that gained from any other event. Le Mans put a

manufacturer's name on the map worldwide.

The Sarthe circuit of more than five miles per lap and an average lap speed of more than 100 mph demanded a high top speed, good acceleration and consistently powerful braking rather than particularly outstanding roadholding. The D-Type was designed with this in mind, and explains why the car was not always so competitive, particularly in later years, over shorter, twistier circuits.

Central to the D-Type's design was its new monocoque centre section.

This 'tub', constructed of 18-ga[u]ge magnesium alloy, gave stren[gth] tempered with lightness. To the fr[ont] bulkhead was argon-arc-welded a s[u]b frame of round and square alumini[um] tubing which carried the front suspension, steering, engine and ancillaries. [At] the rear, a double-skinned bulkhead [was] attached to the live Salisbury rear a[xle] by four trailing arms, two above and t[wo] below the axle. Springing was provi[ded] by a transverse torsion bar and locat[ed] by an A bracket. Front suspension [was] basically similar to the XK's, with [top] and bottom wishbones and longitudi[nal]

1

2

sion bars. Also bolted to the rear khead was the tail section, which was tressed and carried the two flexible tanks and spare wheel. Dunlop disc kes were fitted all round, and newly eloped Dunlop light alloy wheels of her 16- or 17-inch diameter and 5½-h width.

he engine, basically the same XK t with three Weber DCO3 45 mm bs, was mounted at 8° from the verti- and produced 250 bhp at 6000 rpm. e C-Type head was further developed h the enlarging of the inlet valves to inch diameter, and slightly different

camshafts were used. The gearbox was entirely new, being Jaguar designed and all synchromesh. Particularly significant was the fact that the engine now had dry sump lubrication, which reduced the sump depth by half and allowed a lower bonnet line and a better centre of gravity. Axle ratios ranged from 4.09:1 to 2.53:1, the latter making possible a top speed in the region of 200 mph.

The superb body styling was the work of Jaguar's aerodynamicist Malcolm Sayer, and was the result of extensive wind-tunnel testing with one-tenth scale models. Surely a perfect example of the

1 *A typically active, privately campaigned XK 120 belonging to Midlands businessman Bertie Bradnack, seen here with a young Bob Berry at the wheel. Berry later took over from Rankin as head of publicity (B. Bradnack)* 2 *Bertie Bradnack rounding the bottom 'S' at Shelsley (B. Bradnack)* 3 *Practice for the Rheims 12-hour event in which Hamilton (seen here) and Rolt finished second behind Whitehead and Wharton (National Motor Museum)* 4 *OKV 2 was the third D-Type built and had been driven by Moss and Walker at Le Mans (N. Dewis)* 5 *Duncan Hamilton pitting for new goggles in the closing stages of his and Rolt's titanic struggle to catch the leading Ferrari during the very wet 1954 Le Mans race (J C)*

5

'if it looks right, it is right' school of thought, the D-Type had a one-piece, forward tilting, easily removable alloy bonnet, a streamlined head fairing that concealed the fuel filler, and a distinctive fin fitted on the competition cars for straight-line stability.

Curiously, Jaguar's new sports racing car did not gain its name immediately, with the first four cars having XKC chassis numbers (XKC 401–404) and subsequently XKD numbers (XKD 405 and 406 completed the Ds that were built in 1954).

The D-Type's debut at Le Mans in 1954 should have been a glorious one but instead it was a mysterious one. Sabotage has been suggested, but whether this is true or not the fact is that the three D-Types, and only the D-Types, had misfiring problems which were eventually traced to the presence of a fine grey sand in the fuel. Rolt and Hamilton, delayed early on, battled valiantly only to be delayed again when Rolt was forced into a sandbank by another competitor. In spite of this and torrential rain (Hamilton was getting wheelspin at 170 mph), they provided one of the most thrilling finishes ever seen at the French circuit ending up just 105 seconds behind the winning Ferrari of Gonzales and Trintignant.

A little later the tables were turned at the Rheims 12-Hours when Moss destroyed the Ferrari opposition before retiring. Whitehead and Wharton went on to win and Rolt and Hamilton finished second to give Jaguar a fine one-two.

Referring to 1955, Lofty England recalls, 'We managed to acquire the services of one, Hawthorn. A lot more testing was done, more serious preparations carried out and we even flew the cars out to Le Mans.' For 1955, several revised D-Types were built, four of which were retained by the factory (XKD 504/5/6/8) and one was prepared for Briggs Cunningham (XKD 507). Subtle but important changes distinguished these cars from the 1954 cars. For example, XKD 501/2 (both supplied to Ecurie Ecosse at the beginning of 1955) and XKD 503 (similarly supplied to the Belgian national team) and the other 1955 cars had a simplified front sub-frame which was now bolted to the front bulkhead, instead of being welded, to enable easier and speedier repairs. The radiator and oil cooler were mounted on a small subsidiary sub-frame for similar reasons and, most noticeable, the bonnet was lengthened by $7\frac{1}{2}$ inches to improve penetration. The 'long-nose' cars, as they came to be known, had their

wrap-around screens extended back as far as the head fairing to combat buffeting from side winds. More importantly, there were improvements to the cylinder heads in the constant search for more power. The inlet valve diameter was increased to 2 in and the exhaust valve from $1\frac{5}{8}$ in to $1\frac{11}{16}$ in. To avoid valve overlap, the inlet valves were retained at their previous 35° inclination, but that of the exhaust valves was increased to 40°, hence this is known as the 35/40 head or perhaps more generally as the 'wide-angle' head. Power output as a result of

these modifications was raised 275 bhp at 5750 rpm.

Le Mans 1955, saw the D-Type but it was not a victory in which rejoice because it was the year of awful crash. It is sad quite apart from obvious reasons, because the race the makings of a titanic struggle. U the accident, Fangio in the Merce 300SLR and Hawthorn in the long-n D had been having a tremendous c during which Hawthorn set the record at 122.39 mph. Neck-and-n they raced round the long fast circui

Sarthe, swopping places, bringing crowd to their feet and sending the orters into ecstasies. Some have like-1 it to their famous duel in the French and Prix. The Mercedes were with-wn early on Sunday morning and wthorn and Bueb went on to a rather llow victory.

At the TT at Dundrod the Jaguar/ercedes battle was renewed but it led for Hawthorn conclusively when crankshaft broke. 'We didn't think car suitable for the TT at Dunrod Ireland,' recalled England, 'so we just entered one car. We had Hawthorn and Titterington, who lived in Belfast, which kept the expenses down! We were worried about tyre wear for, at Dundrod in 1953, tyres lasted only 35 miles. However, Dunlop had developed a new Stabilio tyre which was steel-braced, and this was much more successful. Anyway, with Moss in the Merc and Hawthorn in the D we were having a good dice when we called Mike in for fuel and a change of tyres. However, to our surprise the tyres were hardly worn, and we sent him out again without

1 Hectic activity during a D-Type night refuelling stop (N. Dewis) 2 Friendly rivals, Moss drove in the team from 1951 to 1954 and Hawthorn in 1955 and 1956 (J C) 3 From very amateur beginnings the famous Scottish team, Ecurie Ecosse, became an increasing force to be reckoned with (N. Baldwin) 4 Grounds hustles his car along in superb scenery during the 1956 Monte, in which another Mark VII, that of Adams, finished first (D. Grounds) 5 The 1955 works cars lined up at Le Mans with Lofty England masterminding affairs. The new longer nose is clearly visible (J C)

5

changing them. A couple of laps later a Mercedes mechanic was holding a sign calling Moss in, when Neubauer rushed forward and bodily picked him up and removed him. Two laps later Moss crashed when a tyre blew. We were very surprised that the normally so ultra-efficient Germans should make a mistake and I mentioned this to chief engineer Uhlenhaut when I met him some months later. He said they hadn't made a mistake, but when we didn't change our tyres they thought their calculations must be wrong!'

The year 1955 saw a class win and fourth overall in the Tulip Rally for the Mark VII, and at the Daily Express meeting Mike Hawthorn led the field to notch up another win. The Monte of that year included a works team of cars driven by Adams, Vard and Appleyard and, although success largely eluded them individually, they collectively won the Charles Farroux Team Trophy. Later in the year a Mark VII won its class in the RAC Rally.

A works team again contested the Monte early in 1956 and this time their reward was outright victory by Adams in his faithful Mark VII. This was perhaps the highspot of the mode illustrious competition career. The y 1955 saw notable private entries such those of Ecurie Ecosse and Dunc Hamilton score wins in D-Types more minor events around the globe.

Six new long-nose cars were built 1956. These differed in various sm details – the most noticeable being provision of a full-width screen to m a change in the regulations for Le Ma Early events provided a series of reti ments and failures rather than success but morale was boosted with factory Types finishing in first, second, a

1

rd places at Rheims.

'At Rheims,' recollects Lofty Eng-
d, 'we had the famous incident when
milton ignored my pit signals. He
ne up to me afterwards and said,
'pose I'm in trouble?" "No trouble at
" I replied, "You just don't drive for
any more!" Some months later at
ristmas he sent me a card and parcel.
ening it I found it contained a mortar
ard and cane. Anyway, some time later
was due at the factory to collect a D
had bought and I told the gate police
ell me immediately he arrived. I knew
would come straight up to my office

and I would have about 30 seconds
warning. I got a phone call to say he had
arrived. I put the mortar board on, took
the cane in my hand and sat down men-
acingly at my desk. At that moment there
was a knock on my door. At my sum-
mons it opened and a commissionaire
walked in. He seemed to find the situation amusing and started to buckle at
the knees. "What's so funny, man. Go
and fetch Mr. Hamilton." When he
returned with Duncan, there were a
number of heads craning to try to see in
through the door!'

Le Mans 1956 was a disaster for the

Jaguar factory but not for the Jaguar
marque. Of the three factory cars, two
crashed on the second lap and the third
was badly delayed with a split fuel line.
But Ecurie Ecosse, those famous
privateers from Scotland, came to the
rescue and Flockhart and Sanderson
drove their D-Type to a fine victory.

The XK140 had even less success in
racing than in rallying for here a trend
had been started some years previously
towards specially designed sports racing
cars rather than specially prepared production sports cars. One of the main
propagators of this had been Jaguar
themselves with the C-Type, and even
more so with the D-Type.

However, a lone XK140 FHC entered
at Le Mans in 1956 far from disgraced
itself. The car, a virtually standard
Special Equipment model with some
25,000 miles recorded, was driven by a
pair of comparatively inexperienced
drivers, Peter Bolton and Bob Walshaw.
The car was prepared by the factory at
a cost of just £1,200 and set off from
home with all tools, spares and supplies
on the roof. At the halfway stage the XK
was lying a most creditable 14th, and as
the hours passed, moved as high as 12th,
beating through reliability and performance, cars with far greater racing pretensions. But with several hours to go the
car was called in by the officials and disqualified for refuelling a lap earlier than
was allowed some hours previously.
This was bitter disappointment but at
least it is on record that the XK140 Fixed
Head covered 1,749 miles at an average
speed of 83 mph. However, I recently
discovered in conversation with a later
owner of the car, that the French had
made a mistake. Bolton and Walshaw
should never have been disqualified and
the French apologized profusely. The
car they probably should have disqualified? None other than the winning
D-Type.

Mike Hawthorn, works driver in 1955
and 1956, seems to have a special place
in Jaguar history because everybody at

2

3

4

1 *The lone 140 FHC of Bolton and Walshaw
that did so well until cruelly disqualified at Le
Mans in 1956* (National Motor Museum) *2
Mike Hawthorn in familiar surroundings with
the famous visor which he preferred to goggles
3 Frank Grounds exercising the suspension of
his Mark 1 saloon during the 1956 RAC Rally*
(D. Grounds) *4 In 1957 Ecurie Ecosse
acquired 1956 works cars. Jack Fairman takes
one of the cars through Becketts at Silverstone*
(J. Fairman)

the factory who knew him remembers him with special affection.

Mike gave the new 3.4 saloon its first victory at the Daily Express meeting at Silverstone in September 1957, being chased by his great friend, and frequent partner-in-crime behind the scenes, Duncan Hamilton. He had several more wins in these cars, racing his own modified road 3.4. Ironically and very tragically he was killed in this car on the Guildford by-pass at the beginning of 1959, having been world champion the previous year and having just announced his retirement from motor racing.

Meanwhile in October 1956, the factory issued the following press release: 'The information gained as a result of the highly successful racing programme which the company has undertaken in the past five years has been of the utmost value, and much of the knowledge derived from racing experience has been applied to the development of the company's products.

'Nevertheless, an annual racing programme imposes a very heavy burden on the technical and research branch of the engineering division, which is already fully extended in implementing plans for the further development of Jaguar cars.

'Although withdrawal from direct participation in racing in the immediate future will afford much needed relief to the technical and research branch, development work on competition cars will not be entirely discontinued, but whether the company will resume its racing activities in 1958 or whether such resumption will be further deferred must depend on circumstances.'

Ironically, 1957 was Jaguar's best year at Le Mans, with the five D-Types entered finishing in first, second, fourth and sixth places. Ecurie Ecosse again provided the winning car, driven by Flockhart and Bueb, and also the second car piloted by Sanderson and Lawrence. The French pair Lucas and Mary were third, the Belgians Frere and Rousselle fourth, and Hamilton and Gregory, although in the fastest car of all, were delayed by the exhaust burning a hole in the floor and had to be content with sixth.

Later in 1957 Ecurie Ecosse were involved in a curious event when the Scottish team were invited to take part in a contest organized at Monza and entitled the Race of Two Worlds. The theory was that it should be a race between a number of American Indianapolis cars and sports cars from Europe over a distance of 500 miles. In practice the event was boycotted by the newly formed International Professional

Driver's Union which excluded all the Europeans bar the Scots, who would have nothing of any boycott.

The D-Types stood no chance of success on the banked bowl against eight Indianapolis cars designed precisely for this form of track. The Ds were restricted to a maximum of 160 mph by problems with tyre temperature after Jack Fairman in practice recalled, 'Just as I was approaching the banking at about 165 mph, the entire right hand back tread came off with a noise like a six-inch shell'.

Because of the bumpy nature of the

track, it was decided to run the event three heats of 166 miles with an hou break between each. The American c gradually fell apart until only three w left. The Ds ran like clockwork a finished a very creditable 4th, 5th a 6th, driven by Fairman (who acqui his nickname of Fearless Jack from event), John Lawrence and Nini Sanderson, respectively.

This was the last D-Type success real importance and, not surprising after four years of racing, they beca less competitive with Lister-Jagu taking over and a three-litre engi

1

2

156

ng mandatory for Le Mans. Such an ine was produced but it never proved able.

he private owners and teams conued as in the previous years to clock innumerable victories and included ong them a young farmer from Scotd named Jim Clark, who drove the der Reivers D-Type to a number of cesses. Clark's career is inseparable m motor racing history and his later ievements are well known, but what perhaps not so familiar is his early olvement with Jaguars.

Clark's first proper season was with

that other Scottish team, the Border Reivers, a group of wealthy young farmers. He drove the team's by then ageing D-Type, TFK 9, and it was during that season that he achieved the first 100 mph lap by a sports car on an unbanked track in this country, and that his team manager Ian Scott-Watson was

1 The year 1957 brought a second victory for Ecurie Ecosse at Le Mans with this D-Type heading the Jaguar domination. Flockhart is in the car with Wilkie Wilkinson on the door and co-driver Bueb on the rear wing (D. Grounds) 2 Wilkie Wilkinson, the Ecurie Ecosse chief mechanic, stands by Jack Fairman awaiting the start of the 1957 Monzanapolis event 3 Fairman completed the 500 miles to finish fourth at an average of 150 mph – probably the highest

average speed in any European event up to that time (J. Fairman) 4 The most successful of all Jaguar-engined sports racing cars was the Lister, seen here in what has come to be known as the 'knobbly' body guise 5 D-Types were still notching up successes in the late 1950s and Jack Fairman corners OKV2, the third D to be built, in a full four-wheel drift at an event in 1958 (J. Fairman)

5

moved to mention in correspondence with Lofty England that they had a young driver in their team of 'extreme promise'.

He later drove the 'flat-iron' Lister Jaguar for the same team, gaining useful international experience

Having built sports cars with MG, Bristol and Maserati engines, with mixed fortunes, Brian Lister was persuaded to copy one of his customers and fit an XK unit. This was the beginning of a successful partnership that was to dominate sports car racing for several years to come in one form or another.

The basis of Lister's design was a chassis formed by two large 3-inch tube side-members and these were cross-braced. Front suspension was by unequal-length wishbones and coil springs, and the rear by a de Dion axle located by four trailing arms and again coil springs. One of the features of a Lister was that the entire body or section thereof could be removed easily in minutes, which must have been appreciated by mechanics.

The new car first appeared in March 1957 piloted by that marvellous driver Archie Scott-Brown, whose name was inseparably linked to that of Lister until his untimely death. Unfortunately, the car had clutch trouble, which ruined chance of winning, but clocking fastest lap was some reward. The meeting produced a win in the Bri Empire Trophy race and the co ination went on to 11 more wins an second out of the 14 races entered season.

Replicas of this ultra-successful began to be built in small number 1958 at a cost of £2,750 plus purch tax, and customers included Ec Ecosse and Briggs Cunningham, was to have a tremendous amount of s cess over the next couple of season the US with his Listers, driven ma

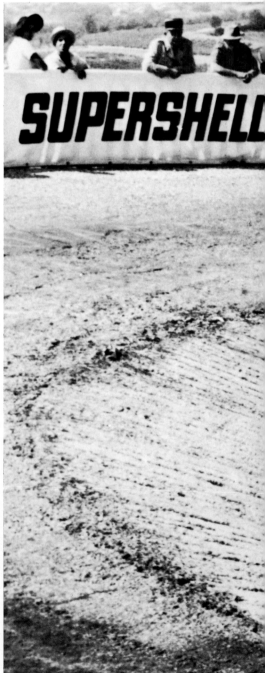

Walt Hansgen.

A single-seater Lister was built to [spe]cial order for Ecurie Ecosse to [cam]paign in a re-run of the previous [year]'s Monzanapolis event. Jack Fair[ma]n drove the car but it broke a valve [in t]he second heat.

[I]n 1958 the wins continued to [acc]umulate, with two Lister works cars, [V]E 303 and VPP 9, being driven by [Sco]tt-Brown (until his tragic death mid-[sea]son), Moss, Hansgen and Bueb. This [ear]ly style, which has come to be known [as t]he 'knobbly' Lister, was superseded [by] a new body designed by aerodynami-[cist] Frank Costin, and these rather more

bulbous cars have come to be known as the Costin bodies.

A few successes came in 1959 but nothing like so many as in the previous two seasons. So, with the gradual emergence of the Cooper and the Lotus rear-engined cars and the lack of competitiveness of the 3-litre version of the XK engine, Brian Lister decided to call it a day at the end of the year.

It would take a complete book to describe all the competition successes of the Mark 1 and 2 models, the racing successes in the UK, in Europe, in other continents such as Australia, the rallying successes everywhere and the records set

up. Perhaps the first of the very long line of triumphs was the Spa Production Touring Car Race in May 1956. Paul

1 *Silverstone 1958, and Mike Hawthorn (VDU 881) and Tommy Sopwith (EN 400) entertain the crowds in their Mark 1 saloons (J C)* 2 *Hawthorn and Sopwith cornering hard during their splendid duel (J C)* 3 *The XK150 was never a serious competition contender but allowed keen club drivers such as Don Smith to have plenty of fun (D. Smith)* 4 *Bernard Consten climbs Mount Ventoux on his way to victory in the 1961 Tour de France, a success he had first achieved in 1960 and one he was to repeat in Mark 2s in 1962 and 1963 (J C)*

Frere, with a modified 2.4, proceeded to win his class and put up best performance irrespective of class, having lapped at 97 mph. The 3.4s took over the mantle of Touring Car supremacy from the Mark VIII, being lighter, and when the Mark 2 3.8s became available, that supremacy was further confirmed.

A long list of successes alone does not make for interesting reading, but a list of some of the more distinguished drivers who have competed in Mark 1s and 2s might. In roughly chronological order they were: Duncan Hamilton, Mike Hawthorn, TEM 'Tommy' Sopwith (who formed a team of Jaguars under the title of Equipe Endeavour), Sir Gawaine Baillie, Ron Flockhart, Walt Hansgen, Ivor Bueb, Roy Salvadori, Jack Sears, Stirling Moss, the late Graham Hill, the late Colin Chapman, Peter Sargent, the late Bruce McLaren, the late Mike Parkes, the late Peter Lindner, Mike Salmon, Mike MacDowel and the late Denny Hulme. Some of the best motor racing seen on television was provided in the early 1960s by the dicing between Graham Hill, Roy Salvadori and Mike Parkes.

In rallying many successes were gained, notably the Morley brothers' class win in the Tulip Rally of 1958 in their 2.4; the winning of the Charles Farroux Team Trophy in the Monte of 1959 by a team of 3.4s; a win overall for the Morleys in the Tulip Rally of the same year, this time in a 3.4; class wins in the 1960 Alpine and RAC rallies; and successive class wins in the Tour de France, including first, second and third places in 1962.

In May 1961, the company was able to advertise: 'For the tenth year, Jaguar wins Silverstone Production Touring Car Race, taking first, second, third, fourth, fifth (all 3.8s) and seventh (2.4) places'. In smaller print it continued, 'since the inauguration in 1949 by the BRDC and the *Daily Express* of the series of International Trophy Meetings at Silverstone, Jaguar cars have achieved

1, 2 *E2A at the factory, just before being taken to Le Mans where it raced in Cunningham's colours. Driven by Walt Hangen and Dan Gurney, it was the fastest in practice but suffered a series of mechanical troubles in the race and finally gave up the ghost after nearly 10 hours (J C)* **3** *The E2A was fitted with a 3.8 engine (note the power bulge) and shipped to the USA, where Cunningham raced it with mixed fortunes (J C)* **4, 5** *The E-Type's first race: Roy Salvadori in the Coombs car, BUY 1, and Graham Hill in the Equipe Endeavour car, ECD 400, leave the pack behind (J C)*

13 consecutive victories in the 13 annual meetings held there including all 10 Production Touring Car Races held annually since 1952'.

In January 1964, a list of the previous year's successes, mostly gained with Mark 2s, necessitated a two-page spread and included Endurance Events (wins in the *Motor* International Six-Hour Touring Car Races, etc.), Long-Distance Records, International Rallies and Touring Car Races (in Australia,

New Zealand, Tasmania, the UK and Germany).

The long-distance records were set up by a team of five drivers led by Geoff Duke at Monza in a 3.8 Mark 2 and International Class C (3000–5000 cc): 10,000 miles at 106.58 mph; 15,000 km at 106.61 mph; 3 days at 107.02 mph; and 4 days at 106.62 mph.

As the company stated in their press release, retirement from racing was only to be temporary. In fact, the factory fire,

an over full order book, and the need devote all available time to develop new replacement production mod meant that Jaguar did not return to ing. Nevertheless, they kept an eye developments at Le Mans, just in c Sir William was quoted as stating, " company has certainly not lost inte in racing. We have not neglected necessary development work for retu ing to the sport. We have made cer plans but just when we will put th

1

operation must depend on
umstances'.

he second development E-Type,
A (A for aluminium) was the logical
elopment of the D-Type, and it had
n intended to run it at Le Mans in
8. Its major difference from the Ds
its independent rear suspension.
er, the car was prised out of Jaguar
Briggs Cunningham and raced by
at Le Mans in 1960. Although it set
fastest time in practice, it lasted only

a few hours in the race, its 3-litre engine
letting it down.

The factory subsequently swopped
the 3-litre unit for a 3.8, and the bonnet
acquired a power bulge. In this form the
Cunningham team campaigned the car
briefly with mixed fortunes. Walt
Hansgen achieved one victory with the
car, but Jack Brabham could not repeat
the result when he drove it.

The E-Type's racing debut was a
fairy-tale one, because a few weeks after

the car had been announced, two completely standard cars were taken to
Oulton Park for a 25-lap GT Trophy
race, where Graham Hill and Roy
Salvadori proceeded to finish first and
third respectively against opposition
that included Aston Martin DB4 GTs
and 250 GT Ferraris.

Three E-Types were privately
entered for Le Mans in 1962 and while
they were not serious contenders for
outright honours, by dint of reliable running they finished fourth and fifth,
driven respectively by Salvadori/
Cunningham and the Peters, Lumsden
and Sargent.

In spite of this and other early successes, the E-Type could not really compete
with the race-bred Ferraris, so some
gradual development of the cars took
place. Notably, the John Coombs semi-
works car, originally registered BUY 1
when raced by Salvadori, but later
changed to 4WPD, came in for constant
attention and modification. A new
monocoque of thinner gauge steel was
substituted and aluminium bonnet was
fitted. The engine was modified and the
suspension gradually developed. The
car raced in this guise in 1962 and, in
spite of a considerable amount of testing
by Hill, although competitive, it was
never outstandingly successful.

It was clear that the Ferrari 250 GTOs
had a considerable weight advantage,
and that if Jaguar wanted the E to be
competitive, that was one of the main
areas for attention. As a result, in late
1962 the factory started to build a few
competition E-Types (they have come to
be known more widely as lightweight Es)
for the coming season. The main difference was the use of an all-aluminium
centre monocoque and aluminium block
for the engine, which also had fuel injection and produced more power than any
other XK unit up to that time. The
engine also featured dry sump lubrication and the D-Type wide-angle head.
The lightening exercise resulted in a saving of some 500 lbs over the standard car

1 *The Competition (lightweight) E-Type pit-
ted against the might of Ferrari at Le Mans
in 1963 (J C)* 2 *Robin Sturgess, one of the first
regularly to race an E-Type, at Silverstone.
This car, the 12th to be built, later appeared
in the film* The Italian Job, *registered
848 CRY (National Motor Museum)* 3 *This
car, one of the trio entered at Le Mans in 1963,
was the most successful, finishing in ninth place
after a variety of adventures (J C)* 4 *In an
effort to improve the drag factor of the E-Type,
Sayer produced this coupé, which Dick Protheroe acquired and used to good effect (J C)*

and approximately 100 lbs over the Ferraris.

These Lightweights, of which about 12 were produced, proceeded to be raced far and wide, including three Briggs Cunningham cars entered at Le Mans. Two of the cars retired but the one registered 5115 WK finished in 9th position. However, apart from a few domestic triumphs, real success again eluded the E-Type drivers, as they came into contention more and more with thinly disguised sports racing cars designed purely with racing in mind.

It is a little sad that these competition modifications were not made earlier in the car's life when it might have covered itself in rather more glory, but the factory at that time had neither the time nor the interest to devote itself wholeheartedly to racing.

Three-times world champion Jackie Stewart had strong Jaguar connections in the early part of his career. Brother Jimmy raced C-Types for Ecurie Ecosse and the two brothers were partners in the garage business started by their father. Dumbuck Motors in Dumbartonshire were Jaguar area dealers and someone once remarked that the arrangement was ideal – ie, Jackie bends them and Jimmy mends them!

In 1962–63, Jackie drove Jimmy's E-Type and said later that it was 'the most forgiving motorcar I have driven . . . you could make it do anything you liked'. As a result of his driving of the E, David Murray picked him to drive the Ecurie Ecosse Tojeiro and Cooper Monaco. This was the beginning of his climb to the heights of Formula One. On the way, he drove Eric Brown's famous XK120 registered 1ALL, and tested and raced the Coombs lightweight E.

Not surprisingly, the trusty XK engine has appealed to a number of specialist builders both for road cars and for racing machines, but mainly for the latter. Sprint specialist Gordon Parker had a series of specials that were Jaguar-powered, notably the Jaguette, fitted with a 1939 SS Jaguar 2½-litre ohv engine; the Jaguara with XK unit; and finally the HK Jaguar with twin superchargers feeding its XK engine. Frank Le Gallais, from Jersey, produced a rear-engined device that had a succession of power units including a 3½-litre Mark 5 unit and ultimately a tuned XK engine.

Oscar Moore fitted an XK unit with great success in his HWM, and the factory followed suit with their sports cars. Another famous name who produced a handful of similarly powered sports racing cars was Cooper. These Cooper

1

2

3

Jaguars, although never outstandingly successful, gained a number of places. Apart from the Listers, dealt with already, the other XK-engined sports car worth noting was the Tojeiro Jaguar, produced in 1956.

In addition to those mentioned, there have been many others, such as Rivers Fletcher's single-seater, Mike Barker's Alton Jaguar, Col Rixon Bucknell's special, the Hansgen Jaguar Special, the Galaxie-engined E-Type called the Egal, various production Panthers in the 1970s, the RGS Atalanta, the RRA Jaguar of Geoff Richardson, the Emeryson-Jaguar and others.

XK engines have enjoyed great success not only on land but also on water. Best known of the record-breaking protagonists was Norman Buckley, who started with an early unit in 1949 adapted for marine use and fitted in his Ventnor Hull. He took the one-hour, three-hour and twenty-hour nautical records. In 1951 with a modified engine, *Miss Windermere II* achieved a mean of 79 mph, and in 1953 and 1954 Buckley, with a different hull, graduated to a C-Type and then to a full three-Webered Le Mans spec. unit.

In 1954, the German von Mayenburg captured the world's eight-hour record with his XK-engined craft. And in 1958 Buckley with his engine now up to D-Type spec, wrested the one-hour record from the German at a speed of 89.08 mph, and with further development was achieving more than 120 mph by 1959. The boat's hull was damaged when dropped from a hoist, so *Miss Windermere IV* was built, this one being a prop-riding hydroplane. Powered by a virtually standard engine from Buckley's 1962 E-Type, a speed of 118.75 mph was achieved in 1970.

Apart from record-breaking boats,

1 *The ultimate sports racing car built by Jaguar, the XJ13, at high speed on the MIRA banking* (N. Dewis) 2 *The heart of the XJ13, its magnificent four overhead cam V12 engine set amidships* (N. Dewis) 3 *There's no mistaking the parentage – the XJ13 was the culmination of the C/D, D-Type, E2A, E-Type theme* (N. Dewis) 4 *Norman Dewis takes the XJ13 out for another run on the MIRA track, the scene of much Jaguar testing over the years* (N. Dewis) 5, 6 *Dewis, who started with XK120s developing disc brakes, nearly finished with the XJ13. Miraculously, the incredibly experienced Dewis escaped relatively unscathed from this monumental shunt, which was probably caused by tyre deflation* (J C)

there have been many well known off-shore racing power boats. John Coombs's boat, named *Cheetah*, was fitted with two 3.8-litre engines. *Tramontana II* and *Jackie S* each boasted a total capacity of 15.2 litres and an output of more than 1000 bhp, with four 3.8 units apiece. The former was owned by Richard Wilkins and driven by Jeffrey Quill, the latter owned and driven by financier Dr Emil Savundra.

The next logical step in Jaguar sports racing car design after E2A was the mid-engined XJ13, the initials standing for 'Experimental Jaguar'. Aware that more power than the six-cylinder engine could

yield would be needed for racing in the 1960s, Jaguar's chose the V12 configuration. The image boost that such an engine would engender was a desirable asset for its eventual use in the production range.

The engine was a four overhead cam unit with a capacity of a fraction under 5 litres. Inevitably in this form it looked rather like two XK heads with a common crankcase. Power output was 502 bhp at 7600 rpm, and it had dry sump lubrication.

Unlike the earlier D and E types, the XJ13 was fully monocoque in construction. It consisted of two main sill boxes

joined by the floor, and a double b head at the front with a single one at rear. To this rear bulkhead was bo the engine, which was stress-bearing carried the transaxle and rear susp sion. At the front, the suspension water and oil radiators were carried another aluminium box section. suspension was basically E-Type the gearbox from ZF.

The bodywork was the work of a dynamicist Malcolm Sayer and a c tinuation of the beautiful D-T theme. Originally, it was planned closed GT car and we can but conject that as such it would have been stag

1

2

3

good looking. Although the XJ13 designed during 1965, it was not pleted until 1966 and was not really d until 1967.

or a variety of reasons Jaguar did not t the press to know that they had a ible Le Mans challenger, and Sir iam gave orders that the car was not e circuit-tested. This eventually me too much for Norman Dewis, discussed it with Lofty England. y in turn said that if Dewis wanted ke it quietly to MIRA one Sunday new nothing about it! This Dewis and several days later was sum- ed to Sir William's office. The con-

versation, according to Norman, went something like this:

Sir William: 'I thought I gave orders that the XJ13 was not to be tested.'
ND: 'Yes you did, sir.'
Sir William: 'And yet you took it to MIRA.'
ND: 'Yes, I did sir.'
Sir William: 'When I give an order I expect it to be obeyed. Don't ever dis-obey me again.'
ND: 'Yessir.'
Sir William: 'Well man, how did it go?'

During 1967, David Hobbs tested the XJ13 round MIRA and set the unofficial record for the fastest lap at any circuit

in Britain, namely, 161.6 mph.

Some time later, a tyre blew out while Dewis was going round MIRA and the car somersaulted, luckily without serious injury to the driver, but with considerable injury to the car. Fortunately, Abbey Panels still had the

1 *Bob Tullius in the Group 44 prepared V12 E-Type leading one of its main rivals, which he continually defeated in spite of being outnumbered (J C)* 2 *Schenken and Rouse lead from the start of the 1977 TT at Silverstone, but as usual it was not to last (J C)* 3 *The Group 44 V12 XJS in Trans-Am action with 1979 champion Bob Tullius driving (J C)*

body formers, so the car could be rebuilt.

On reflection, it is very sad that the XJ13 was not developed more rapidly because many feel that it could have beaten the GT40s and regained for Jaguar the supremacy they had enjoyed in the 1950s.

With regard to body styling, the late Malcolm Sayer's influence on the Jaguar line was second only to that of 'the old man'. He joined the company as a trained aerodynamicist and was responsible for the C-Type, the development C/D prototype and his most famous design, the D-Type. From the original car he evolved the famous long nose and fins of various shapes and sizes. He must have been one of the first to apply aircraft principles to sports racing car design based on his close connections with the Royal Aircraft Establishment at Farnborough, and their wind tunnel.

Sir William liked to work with a full-scale mock-up, but Sayer preferred to draw his cars full-scale on the wall, working out every detail in theory first. Although the influence of his designs for a road-going mid-engined car can be seen in the current XJS, his *pièce de résistance* must surely be the XJ13, the climax of the Jaguar racing line and whose styling he was responsible for.

In mid-1974 Bob Tullius of Group 44 persuaded BL that the ageing V12E could be raced successfully in Category B sports car events in the US, and that this would give a fillip to dropping sales. BL agreed and commissioned Group 44 of Virginia and Huffaker Engineering of California to cover their respective coasts. The results were impressive. Huffaker won first time and Group 44

finished the season, which for them started in August, as Northeast Divi Champions with five victories and se track records from seven starts.

The following year was similarly s cessful, with ten starts netting seven tories and eight track records, enab Tullius to become SCCS Natic Champion.

The racing XJ Coupés were built raced in 1976 and 1977, just two seas in which they at times showed their tastic potential, but sadly never real it by winning any event. Some say they were not given sufficient time prove themselves. We shall never kn

The cars, prepared to FIA Grou regulations applicable to the Europ Touring Car Championship, were fi with 5416 cc fuel-injected V12 eng developing more than 530 bhp. Init

1

ey used a wet sump lubrication but
ter changed to a dry sump system.
ather controversially, the cars were
uilt and prepared not by the factory but
y Broadspeed, independent of the
ctory.

The first year, 1976, was an embar-
ssing one for all concerned, because
ritish Leyland, who had announced the
r with a fanfare of publicity long before
was properly developed, had very red
ces when the cars repeatedly failed to
art.

The following year was more success-
l, with a second place at Nürburgring
d pole position at every event bar one.
ime and again the Leylands (not Jagu-
s) proved to be considerably quicker
an their main rivals the BMWs, but
ey just could not last the distance at the
ice.

For a while the Coupés provided a
great spectacle, making what would
otherwise have been a dull championship more exciting. It is sad that they
could not have earned just a little glory.
Derek Bell, one of the regular team
drivers, told me recently, 'I enjoyed the
cars, and they could have been very good
if they had been persevered with a little
longer'.

In the States, luckily things went very
much better. Towards the end of 1976
Group 44 switched to an XJS and won
a Sports Car Club of America race at
Lime Rock. The engine in this car produced 475 bhp aided by no less than six
Webers and dry sump lubrication.

In 1977 Group 44 entered the Trans
Am Championship and won five out of
ten Category One races, beating Porsches and Chevrolet Corvettes in the pro-

cess, with the V12 now developing
536 bhp. This gave the car a 0–60
acceleration time of 5 seconds, with
100 mph coming up in a further 5.3
seconds, and a top speed of around
190 mph. Weight was reduced by
240 lbs by fitting a fibreglass bonnet and
plexi-glass rear window. These wins
plus a second and third gave Tullius and
Group 44 the Category One championship. The following year was similarly
successful, with Tullius and Group 44
taking the driver's and manufacturer's
titles.

1 'Jaguar back in racing' ran the headlines, and
what better sequel than 'Jaguar wins at
Donington'? (J C) 2 After a fine drive by
Martin Brundle in awful conditions, this was
the view seen by the opposition at the end of the
Donington race (J C)

In 1982 the highly respected race car preparation company, Tom Walkinshaw Racing (TWR), prepared an XJS for racing in Australia and in doing so had the idea that it would make an ideal basis for tackling the BMWs in the European Touring Car Championship, Group A sector. With backing from Motul, a French oil firm, and the approval of Jaguar, TWR set out to do just that. Entering the fray mid-season they bagged four wins, including a first and second at the TT at Silverstone. This was the first Jaguar victory in this most historic event since Moss's win in a C-Type in 1951.

Impressed by the professionalism of the team and the unquestionable success gained, Jaguar felt able to come out in the open and officially back the team as official entrants. Thus Jaguar were back in racing (XJCs had been entered as Leylands or whatever, not as Jaguars) after 26 years.

The philosophy of Group A is that a car's major areas must in principle be unaltered from their production counterparts. Bodywork must remain unaltered and suspension principles must be adhered to, with the aim of proving the inherent ability, or lack of same, of a car's design, rather than to accept thinly disguised racing cars that bear no relation to the standard product.

The TWR XJS was given an engine developing 400 bhp as opposed to the standard 299. Walkinshaw commented that they could get 500 bhp but the consumption would be a problem, because the extra fuel stops would cancel out any speed advantage. With a top speed in the region of 170 mph and a weight of almost 1½ tons, braking was also a potential problem. To overcome this, 13-inch ventilated discs were fitted all round those at the rear being mounted outbound.

In 1983 the results came gradually. In the first race at Monza, one of the two team cars finished second by 3½ seconds after the bonnet had come loose and a stop had to be made to tape it down. A third followed at Vallelunga. At Donington, young Martin Brundle put in a stirring drive in heavy rain to snatch a superb victory. Further victories were gained and at the year end the score stood at BMW 6, Jaguar 5, a worthy feat when one considers that the two XJS were taking on more than a dozen BMWs.

Meanwhile in the USA, Group 44 had not been resting on their laurels. Th

1

Js had been further developed, parcularly in the engine department, and ad gained three Trans Am wins in 1981. ut these engine developments were tended for something even more xciting.

Jaguar, now with its new enlightened adership, had expressed a desire to mpete in a world series rather than in purely domestic one. Hence the idea of uilding a purpose-designed prototype ith the Jaguar V12 engine powering it. obody would admit it although it was nted at, but Jaguar's old stomping ound – where a certain 24-hour event ok place in France – was at the back their minds.

As a result, a striking GT prototype s designed by American Lee Dykstra r Tullius. It was an aluminium Honeymb monocoque design with steel bulk-heads and the V12 mounted amidships. The fibreglass bodywork enclosed a design along ground-effect principles then current in Formula One. The car was initially intended for the American IMSA series, but was built with long-distance endurance events in mind. The XJR-5, as it was known, gained several wins in the USA in 1983 and in 1984 it was decided to enter Le Mans, more as an experiment than a serious attempt to win. With Brian Redman now a team member and John Watson joining for Le Mans, the cars far from disgraced themselves against the sheer weight of Porsches.

For 1984 TWR added a third car plus former ETC champion Hans Heyer and proceeded to dominate the Series. By round 6, the halfway mark, they had amassed 5 wins and on two occasions a 1st, 2nd and 3rd. Such was the new enthusiasm for competition that Sales and Marketing Director, Neil Johnson, stated that sales had risen as a result and that racing had 'greatly contributed to our reputation for quality. Jaguar's name,' he concluded, 'can only be enhanced by a professionally run racing programme'.

1 *The XJR-5 underwent considerable development in 1982 and 1983 – the few races entered were regarded as tests only (*J C*)* **2** *The stylish V12-engined XJR-5. Driving in 1982 and 1983 was shared by Tullius and Canadian Bill Adam (*J C*)* **3** *The XJR-5 certainly looks very different from a D-Type but will it emulate its famous ancestor? (*J C*)*

2

3

The second half of the '84 season was not quite so dominant a one for the TWR XJSs, though it did include a famous victory in the old-established Spa 24–hour classic, and the amassed results were sufficient to bring Tom Walkinshaw the title of European Touring Car Champion.

With the occasional exception, the cars now entered honourable retirement as TWR moved up a league or two and took on the challenge of Le Mans. This was a rather different game and involved not merely modifying an existing production car but designing and building a state of the art sports racing car to take on the might of established and vastly experienced teams such as Porsche and Lancia.

The responsibility for design was given to Tony Southgate, an ex-Formula One man with wide experience. During this period the British undoubtedly led the world in chassis design and the effective use of ground effects. The new XJR–6 was no exception, and by cleverly using venturi tunnels together with rear spats to increase effectiveness, the ground effect and resultant downforce of this Kevlar and composite honeycomb chassis were superior to that of its rivals.

However, this was essential for the Porsches had more power and being turbo-charged gave them the option to turn up the boost for short periods to, for example, set a fast practice time or carry out an overtaking manoeuvre. The Jaguars, with their normally aspirated six-litre V12 engines did not have that option but, without turbo lag, the cars were far easier to drive and in the wet, the extra downforce became [a] particularly advantageous factor.

Meanwhile in the U.S.A., Group [A] were picking up a smattering of plac[es] with the XJR–5s. Notable resul[ts] included a 3rd in the Daytona 24–ho[ur] event, an excellent 1st and 2nd [at] Miami and 2nds at Charlotte, Portlan[d] Sears Point, Pocono and a three-ho[ur] event at Daytona. These results, to[o] gether with the three 3rds, netted th[e] team 3rd position in the Manufacturer[s] Chassis and Engine Championship.

Although the XJR–6s we[re] completed in time for Le Mans '8[5] they were not considered to be suff[i]ciently tested and developed to moun[t a] worthwhile showing and it was left to [a] couple of XJR–5s from the State[s] based team to represent the Briti[sh] marque. Unfortunately neith[er]

1

tinguished itself. In their own coun-
the enthusiastic Group 44 team,
to feel their efforts did not always
ceive whole-hearted support from
ventry, could again only manage a
gle win, this time at Road Atlanta,
d a handful of 2nds, 3rds and 4ths. In
ite of this the team finished a place
gher in the Manufacturers' Cham-
onship, and team driver, Chip Robin-
n, took 5th place in the Drivers'
ampionship.

Their concluding event of the season
d seen the debut of the completely
w XJR–7 which finished 4th, while
older XJR–5 in the hands of Hurley
ywood and Brian Redman missed a
n by the slender margin of just eight
onds.

Late in 1985 the new XJR–6s entered
fray and looked promising even if

lacking power. In their first event
Martin Brundle and Mike Thackwell
actually led before finishing third. At
Spa at the beginning of September, the
same duo finished in a lowly fifth
position but the team ended the season
on a high note with a second clocked up
by Thackwell/Nielsen/Lammers at
Selangor.

In October the TWR XJSs were
dusted down, brought out of retirement
and shipped to Australia. The James
Hardie 1000 at Bathurst is, arguably,
the toughest and most famous road race
in the southern hemisphere. The scale
of TWR's challenge is illustrated by the
fact that it had been won on the last
eighteen successive occasions by
Australian-built Fords and Holdens.

One of the three TWR cars dropped
out early on with engine trouble but the

other two piloted by Tom Walkinshaw
and Win Percy, and Armin Hahne and
local hero, John Goss, held a healthy
1–2 for several hours. Towards the end
the leading Walkingshaw car had to pit
twice with a damaged oil cooler. This
delay meant that they finished only
third, but the other car took the
chequered flag ahead of the rest for a

1 *With three TWR XJSs running in 1984,
they established a firm supremacy over their
main rivals, the BMWs, and Tom
Walkinshaw ended the season as European
Touring Car Champion.* **2** *In 1985 TWR
graduated to sports car racing with a new
state-of-the-art ground effects car designed by
Tony Southgate.* (Jaguar Cars)

splendid win.

For 1986 the previously British Racing Green TWR Jaguars were to have a new livery, for it was announced that Gallaher International were to sponsor the team of three cars in the colours of their Silk Cut cigarette brand. Such are the astronomic costs of racing today that commercial reality dictates outside contributions, but nevertheless it is sad that the Jaguars had to forsake their traditional, patriotic colours in return for those of a cigarette packet.

Concentrated efforts over the winter brought the weight of the XJR-6 down to just over the 850 kg. limit, and the V12 engines were modified to give both better power and more torque. The team, it was announced, was to be led by Grand Prix drivers, Derek Warwick and Eddie Cheever.

Although the first event of the season was a sprint one and suited the turbo-charged cars better, this duo gained an excellent victory at Silverstone in May. The Martini-Lancias were fastest in practice, but after leading, the Italian car had electrical trouble and allowed the Anglo-American pair to top the leaderboard ahead of the Rothmans Porsche of Bell and Stuck.

The next round was the big one – Le Mans. It seems that the kudos and publicity engendered by this single event outweighs the total of all the other rounds put together. With this in mind, Southgate designed a new body specifically for the constant high speeds attained and maintained at the French classic. The results of wind-tunnel testing, computer calculations and practical testing at the Le Mans test day

in May, led to a body which was sligh longer at the rear and had the rear wi mounted much lower to reduce drag

However, the event was not a hap one for the Jaguars and all three retir The first dropped out due to failing fi pressure, the second broke a half-sh whilst travelling at 220 mph on t Mulsanne Straight and the third s fered a high speed puncture. T flailing rubber severely damaged t adjacent body work and preclud continuance.

The rest of the season did not particularly well, though Warwick a Lammers very nearly caught t winning Porsche of Boutsen a Jelinski at the 1000 kms event at S Francorchamps. Both cars were f tering due to a lack of fuel. The f places gained by Derek Warwick me

1

it he went to the final round at Fuji
th an outside chance of taking the
ivers' Championship. By finishing
rd, and not second as was first
nounced, he cruelly missed it by a
int.

Meanwhile in the U.S. Group 44 did
t achieve any wins in 1986 until the
t event but consistent placing gained
em the second spot in the Manufac-
ers' Championship once more. The
cluding event was the Eastern
lines 3-hour event at Daytona and
XJR-7 took its first win, with Bob
llius and Chip Robinson at the helm.
was announced that for 1987 the team
d decided to concentrate on develop-
nt rather than competition.

The year, 1987, turned out to be an
ellent one for the TWR team and the
ised design which was now known as

the XJR-8. Over sixty detail changes
had been made to the 1986 cars and the
latest cars were lighter, stiffer, more
powerful and had even greater
downforce than their predecessors.

The season began in blistering fashion with victories in each of the first
four rounds. New recruit, John Watson, and Jan Lammers took rounds one
and three at Jarama in Spain and
Monza, respectively. Rounds two and
four saw team-mates Eddie Cheever
and Raul Boesel victorious at Jerez and
Silverstone, but the next event was the
one that Jaguar really wanted to win.

Three XJR-8LM cars were built and
entered for Le Mans. For a number of
hours the cars were on the pace and in
the leading pack, but gradually the
gremlins began to attack the British
cars. After 10 hours, 40 minutes Win

Percy, in the car he was sharing with
Lammers and Watson, had the most
unpleasant experience of a tyre explod-
ing at 200 mph plus. The car flew
upside-down for some distance and it is
a credit to Tony Southgate that Percy
survived, let alone walked away.

With fifteen hours gone the Martin
Brundle and John Nielsen car was

1 *However the new XJR-6 was not considered to be ready for Le Mans and Jaguar
were once more represented by Group 44.*
(Jaguar Cars) 2 *In 1987 TWR designed and
developed a new car, the XJR-9, and had an
excellent season though the 'jewel in the
crown', the prestigious Le Mans win still
eluded them.* (Philip Porter)

running in second spot when it had to retire with a cracked cylinder head. This allowed the third car to inherit the second position but a traumatic period followed when it was beset by gearbox problems, necessitating a rebuild, electrical bothers, which caused the car to halt on the circuit, as did fuel-feed trouble and, finally, a rear suspension upright had to be changed. In a race of attrition the car, driven by Cheever, Boesel, and latterly, Lammers still managed to finish in fifth place.

It is difficult to escape the fact that weight of numbers wins Le Mans. A large number of the Porsches hit trouble very early on but the fact that there were so many competing allowed the marque to still occupy the first two positions. Three Jaguars was just not enough.

The Porsches dominated the results of round six at the Norisring in Germany. This unpopular event was run in two heats, one heat to be driven by each driver. Whilst leading his heat, Lammers had a differential failure and poor old 'Wattie' did not even get a race. Boesel won the second heat, but as Cheever had only managed 13th, as a result of low fuel pressure, fifth was the result on aggregate.

The circus then returned to Britain for round seven at Brands Hatch. The result was rather better for Jaguar supporters with Boesel/Nielsen winning and Lammers/Watson finishing third. Cheever and Boesel won the next event in Germany, at the famous Nurburgring and thus the Silk Cut Jaguar team annexed the World Championship for Group C sports-prototypes.

For the next race at Spa, TWR added a third car for Martin Brundle and Johnny Dumfries. The result, after opposition in the form of the Brittan-Lloyd Porsche 962 of Palmer and Baldi, and the Kouros Sauber Mercedes of Thackwell and Schlesser, had fallen by the wayside, was that the Jaguars finished 1st, 2nd and 4th. With Boesel, electing to take a stint in the leading car late in the race, he duly won the Drivers' Championship.

Towards the end of '87 Jaguar decided to cease their involvement with Group 44. Ironically the year had yielded two excellent victories with Hurley Haywood and John Morton taking the single XJR-7 to the chequered flag at Riverside and Palm Beach. It was rather sad to see the end of the Group 44 Jaguar connection. The team had done a superb job with the ageing V12 E-types and the Trans

Am XJSs, and whilst the sports racing cars did not bring a rash of victories, the team always put on a superbly professional show against difficult odds.

Late in the year it was announced that TWR would be setting up an American operation and running a team of their cars in the IMSA Championship with sponsorship from Castrol. As the TWR team finished its year with an excellent one-two in Japan, it was further announced that Martin Brundle would be rejoining the team for 1988.

For 1988 the faithful Southgate design was further revised and henceforth known as the XJR-9. The season opened with a second place for Nielsen, Watson and new recruit, Andy Wallace to the team that looked like being the main opposition for the year, the Sauber Mercedes. However, winning form was regained by the Jaguars thereafter with team leaders, Brundle and Cheever clocking up victories at Jarama, Monza and Silverstone.

For Le Mans, TWR entered no less

than five XJR-9LMs and the odds we improved as a consequence. They we further improved when the two Saub Mercedes were withdrawn during pra tice after Klaus Niedzwiedz had su fered a burst tyre just before t Mulsanne Kink. The three facto Porsches turned up the boost in pra tice and took the first three g positions with Brundle fourth fastest

Within 25 minutes Lammers was the lead in the fastest of the Jagu followed by the three Porsches a Brundle. After driver changes Niels suffering from bad handling in t Brundle car, spun into the sand trap Indianapolis Corner and lost a lap bei towed out. The leading Porsche w delayed when Ludwig stayed out for lap longer than he should have a virtually ran out of fuel losing two la in the process.

During the early evening t Lammers/Dumfries/Wallace Jagu battled with the Wollek/Schuppan/V der Merwe Porsche, followed by t Andretti Porsche and Jaguars

Sullivan/Cobb/Jones and Boesel/Watson/Pescarolo. The fifth Jaguar, that of Daly/Cogan/Perkins had been delayed when Cogan spun under the Dunlop Bridge.

In the twelfth hour the Wollek Porsche left the fray with engine problems but the Stuck/Ludvig/Bell Porsche was making up for the ground lost earlier and moved up to second spot. The Brundle car was back up to third, but Boesel had had to abandon his car on the circuit with a broken transmission and the Sullivan car was way back having lost 50 laps as a result of two long stops to change the rear end once in an effort to eradicate a severe transmission vibration.

Meanwhile the Lammers Jaguar maintained its lead losing it only briefly whilst pitting for a new windscreen. The Stuck Porsche also suffered a delay having a new water pump fitted and the Jaguar now had a cushion of one lap. During Sunday morning the Brundle car dropped out with head gasket failure.

Having had to push the Stuck/Ludvig/Bell Porsche to make up for the time lost early on, the drivers had to drive to conserve fuel later in the race and this prevented them from mounting a late charge. The result was that the Jaguar of Jan Lammers, Johnny Dumfries and Andy Wallace crossed the line to take Jaguar's sixth Le Mans win with two minutes to spare. Apart from the Derek Daly Jaguar in fourth place, the rest of the top ten positions were occupied by Porsches and the Sullivan XJR-9 came home in 16th position.

The Brundle/Nielsen partnership was more successful at Brno in Czechoslovakia and at Brands Hatch where they finished in second and first positions respectively. At the Nurburgring Brundle was teamed once more with Cheever and second place was the result, as it was for Brundle and Lammers at Spa. To conclude a superb season, the circus moved away from Europe and Brundle/Cheever won at Fuji and finished in third spot at Sandown in Australia.

All these excellent results meant that Jaguar and Martin Brundle demonstrably won their respective crowns, the Manufacturers' and Drivers' World Championships.

Meanwhile the American TWR team had been involved in a busy schedule of IMSA events and Brundle had been frantically jetting to and fro to spearhead that effort as well. The year began and ended with wins but the 12 races in between yielded just a number of places.

When I discussed Jaguar's racing involvement with Sir John Egan, back in late '86, he had this to say. 'Jaguar is expected to go racing and is expected to be competitive. One of the things that does concern me, however, about racing, is the instability of the rules and regulations. But we have enjoyed our racing and I think it has reflected well on the company. The racing programmes have put some money back into our "image bank".'

The 1989 season was a transitional period for both the Silk Cut Jaguar team competing in the World Sports Prototype series and the Castrol Jaguar team tackling the Camel IMSA GTP Championship in the States. The nature of the World Championship races was changing with some of the longer traditional endurance races becoming more akin to short sprint races. These did not suit the V12 powered XJR-9 as well as the more nimble competition. In the States the XJR-9 was heavily revised to suit local conditions rather than the World series tracks it had been designed for.

The season started well in the States with Price Cobb and John Nielsen scoring their second successive IMSA second place in the three-hour Miami G. P. The same pairing scored the same result at the 37th annual Sebring 12-hour race and at this stage Jaguar led the championship from Nissan and Porsche, but the Jaguar challenge faded from hereon.

At Le Mans the four XJR-9LMs were dogged by a series of irritating

1 In 1988, at the third attempt, TWR increased the number of Jaguar's Le Mans victories from five to six with the special Le Mans-bodied XJR9 LM taking the spoils (Jaguar Cars) 2 Also in 1988 TWR established a new U.S. base and IMSA version of the XJR-9 to contest the American series with backing from Castrol. (Jaguar Cars) 3 Though not quite so successful in the States, the TWR team had a superb season in the world series and team leader, Martin Brundle, ended the season as the 1988 World Sports Car Champion. (Jaguar Cars)

misfortunes and could do no better than fourth and eighth places behind the season-dominating Sauber Mercedes. A record fastest lap by Alain Ferte in the Jaguar was the only consolation.

In mid-season TWR introduced two new race cars based around a new twin turbo-charged V6 engine entitled the JV-6. This was to be raced in 3.5-litre form in the World series and 3.0-litre configuration in the States. Intended for the 1990 season and beyond, the debut had to be accelerated due to changes in regulations which effectively outlawed the engine from 1991 onwards. The new XJR-10 finished in second place in its first US race at Lime Rock and the XJR-11 made its debut in World events, showing both great promise and the need for further development.

While the V6-powered cars were designed for the shorter races, it was believed that the V12-engined cars s[..] had a part to play in the endura[..] races. Hence the XJR-9 was heav[..] revised and renamed the XJR-12 for [..] 1990 season. It could not have star[..] better. The two Jaguars took the fi[..] two places in the Daytona 24-hour ra[..] America's toughest, after a nine h[..] dice with the leading Nissan and [..] strong challenge from Porsche. An [..] Wallace, Jan Lammers and Davy Jo[..]

aded home team mates Brundle,
ielsen and Cobb.

At Suzuka Brundle nearly took a fine
cond place but the engine blew with
e laps to go and at Monza they
ished third and fourth behind the all-
nquering Mercedes. Back on home
l the Jaguars reversed the tables and
ok a superb one-two at Silverstone.
e XJR-10 scored a win at Lime Rock
d, back in Europe, Lammers and

4 In 1990 *Jaguar recorded their seventh Le Mans
victory with an impressive first and second
placing, the winning car being handled by
Britain's Martin Brundle, Denmark's John
Nielsen and America's Price Cobb – a truly
international trio.* (J C) 5 *The beautiful XJR-15
was created for what was billed as 'the ultimate
one-make series'. It consisted of races at three of*

*the leading European GPs with a million dollar
prize fund.* (J C) 6 *The radical* 1991 *XJR-14
was effectively a state-of-the-art Formula One
car with a sports car body, and totally dominated
the* 1991 *season earning for Jaguar another
World Championship crown and for Teo Fabi the
drivers' title.* (J C)

5

6

Wallace took a hard-fought second at Spa. Drama was caused in practice at Le Mans with the withdrawal of the Mercedes team after one of the cars had experienced an unexplained puncture at high speed.

Once again four Jaguars were entered and, though they did not set the pace in the early stages, the *hares* gradually fell by the wayside. 'We knew', stated Team Manager Tom Walkinshaw, 'that we would have to grind the opposition into the ground and break them and that's what we did.' With the Japanese Nissan challenge gone and the German Porsche challenge blunted, the leading XJR-12 of Nielsen and Cobb took the lead as dawn broke. Brundle, whose car had been sidelined with a faulty water pump, joined the leading crew and captivated the crowd with a fine display of sprint driving as he held off a hard charging Oscar Larrauri in the Brun Porsche. When this car cruelly broke down with just 14 minutes of the race left, the XJR-12 of Wallace, Lammers and Franz Konrad inherited second spot, to record a splendid one-two in the world's most famous sports car race.

The second half of the 1990 season was a frustrating one for Jaguar in both championships with a number of places being gained, but the cars just fractionally off the pace. However TWR designer Ross Brawn was working on a completely new car for the 1991 season and in October it was announced that Formula One star Derek Warwick would be rejoining the Silk Cut Jaguar team.

Further announcements included the launch by JaguarSport of an exclusive one-make racing series with a million dollar prize fund. The three races making up the series were to support three of Europe's most prestigious races, the Grand Prix of Monaco, Britain and Belgium. For this series TWR had designed and built a completely new car, the XJR-15. A maximum of 30 identical cars would make up the grid. The car stemmed from Project R9R, a concept car developed by JaguarSport as a means of testing the application of carbon composite materials and plastics in high performance vehicle construction. Based on the 1988 Le Mans winning XJR-9, the XJR-15 was powered by a 450 bhp version of JaguarSport's 6.0-litre V12 engine with an advanced electronically controlled managed fuel injection system.

For the 1991 World Sportscar Championship TWR unveiled a radical new challenger to meet the new regulations which outlawed turbo-charged engines. Powered by a normally aspirated V8 engine, developed specifically by Cosworth for Jaguar, the new car drew heavily on the current Formula One design technology. Externally the car looked like a sports car, but under the aerodynamic bodywork was effectively a two-seater Formula One chassis. This latest car was named the XJR-14.

The first round was at Suzuka and the Jaguars immediately proved themselves faster than rivals Mercedes and Peugeot. At one stage Warwick and Brundle held the first two places but then Martin fell out with dropping fuel pressure and Warwick was delayed when the engine refused to restart following a pitstop. Over in the States the Jaguar team, now sponsored by Bud Light, won the Miami GP with Raul Boesel at the wheel.

The next World series round at Monza was a race of see-sawing fortunes for all the main contenders. In practice the Jaguars once again totally dominated the opposition from Mazda, Mercedes-Benz, Peugeot and Porsche. After a last minute engine change, Brundle had to start from the pit lane, and thus last, but by the third lap he was in third place with Fabi in the other XJR-14 leading. After a succession of problems, the race concluded with the Jaguars of Warwick/Brundle and Fabi/Brundle – Martin having done stints in both cars – in the two leading positions. Over in the States the XJR-10

was succeeded by the new XJR-16 a[nd] totally dominated its debut race, t[he] Grand Prix of Atlanta, taking victory [by] more than a minute.

The domination experienced [by] the XJR-14 at Silverstone was su[ch] that they were nearly four secon[ds] faster in practice than the next quicke[st] the Peugeots. In the race Brundle, w[ho] was driving solo, was delayed by [a] broken throttle cable and dro[ve] brilliantly to take third positio[n.] Meanwhile his team mates Warwick a[nd] Fabi had walked away from the fie[ld] and finished two laps ahead of t[he] second-placed Mercedes driven by tw[o] young men called Karl Wendlinger a[nd] Michael Schumacher. Annoying[ly] Warwick was docked his points becau[se] he had been nominated for the oth[er] car.

Jaguar relied once more on t[he] venerable 7.4-litre V12 XJR-12 cars f[or] Le Mans and they nearly brought hom[e] the bacon. The Peugeot and Merced[es] challenges fell apart but Jaguar we[re] thwarted by the rotary-engin[ed] Mazdas which had been given [a] favourable low minimum weig[ht] on which they could race, there[by] assisting their fuel consumption. Th[e] cause was also helped by a very fi[ne] drive from Johnny Herbert. The Jagua[rs] finished in second, third and four[th] places.

At the Nurburgring the TWR tea[m] beat a three-year German jinx and swe[pt] to a convincing one-two result wi[th] Warwick and Fabi/Brabham finishi[ng]

7

less than six laps ahead of the third-[pla]ced Porsche.

[T]he circus moved to Magny Cours in [Fra]nce in September where Peugeot [use]d their local knowledge to good [effe]ct and took the first two places, with [Teo] Fabi and David Brabham in third. [In] Mexico City Jaguar clinched their [thi]rd World Championship in five [yea]rs, though it was not a very [sati]sfactory race. Fabi non-started with [an] engine oil system fault and Warwick [had] a massive spin when it suddenly [rain]ed. Having changed to wet tyres, he [dro]ve superbly to work his way up to [sec]ond when, with the track drying, he [opt]ed once more for slicks and had a [star]ter motor problem which delayed [hin] for five laps. He finished sixth. At [the] final race at the new Autopolis [cir]cuit in Japan Warwick was second [and] Fabi/Brabham were third, sufficient [to] give Teo Fabi the World Drivers' [Ch]ampionship by seven points from [De]rek Warwick.

[M]eanwhile in the States the Jaguars [had] been the cars to beat and had won [ten] of the first 13 races to compare with [thr]ee wins by Nissan, two by Toyota and [one] apiece for Chevrolet-Intrepid and [Lo]la.

[A]fter a brief hiatus, Jaguar returned [to t]he competition world in 1993 with [the] fabulous XJ220 supercar. [Jag]uarSport, in conjunction with TWR [Rac]ing, prepared several cars for GT [rac]ing. Unfortunately a variety of ever [cha]nging rules did not make an [attr]active package to entice

manufacturers and teams to enter, and GT racing always seems to have struggled to realise its, surely, immense potential.

A competition version, appropriately named the XJ220C, was shown at the Auto Sports International show at the Birmingham's NEC in January 1993 and Walkinshaw announced that examples could be bought for £380,000. A brace of 220s were prepared for the Italian Group N series and it was these that actually made the model's debut. The XJ220C's first British appearance took place at Silverstone in May when Win Percy drove a single entry and demolished the opposition.

'It was more of a demonstration run to be honest', he told me. 'Although the opposition, the Porsches, had far more power, the fact that this was a modern era motor car really showed up against the braking and cornering speeds of the Porsches and Aston Martin.'

Three XJ220Cs, painted in Scottish blue, were prepared and entered for the 1993 Le Mans race. Practice was marred by controversy when, as has so often happened to British cars at Le Mans over the years, the officials tried to disqualify the Jaguars. They were allowed to run under appeal and, after many mishaps, the example driven by John Nielsen, David Brabham and David Coulthard won the GT class, or did it? It certainly won on the road but some weeks later was excluded from the results on the grounds that TWR had not lodged their appeal in time!

It is not a happy epitaph to Jaguar's great competition record, but hopefully there will be more chapters to write in the future. Motor racing made the company's reputation and it is to be hoped that the proud cat will return again to uphold, and strengthen, the sporting image which has done so much to make a great name known and respected throughout the world.

7 *With the Cosworth V8-engined XJR-14 designed for the relatively, shorter races, the V12-engined XJR-12 was retained and used most effectively for the long distance, endurance races such as Daytona and Le Mans.* (JC) 8 *In 1993 Jaguar and TWR returned to Le Mans with a C-type, the XJ220C, some 40 years after the original XK120C had recorded its second great win. The new 'C' took a good win in the GT class, until disqualified by French officialdom!* (J C)

12 STYLING THEMES

The 'Lyons line' is a famous phrase in motoring circles and is confirmation that this first-rate businessman also influenced the design of most of his products very heavily. Also, we should not forget the part that the highly respected aerodynamicist Malcolm Sayer played in literally helping to shape the range by applying principles learnt in competition design and development.

1

ore World War II, William Lyons
ded to follow contemporary fashion
produced cars with long low bonnets
Bentley-type styling. But after the
it was another matter. Lyons led
ion, 'daring', as the adverts put it, 'to
boldly individual'. But where did his
uences come from? It is interesting
note the similarity between certain
dels of Bugatti and later Jaguars. This
uld not be taken as criticism of
ons's work, but rather as a hint as to
ere part of his inspiration may have
n derived.

The Type 57 Bugatti in two of its
many forms provides a couple of interesting comparisons. The T57S in
Atalante guise has many similarities to
the XK120 Fixed-head of approximately
20 years later. The relative positioning
of headlamps, sidelights, grille and bonnet profile are very similar, and in side
view silhouette the 120 is a development
of Jean Bugatti's theme – first seen as
a Lyons theme in the one-off SS100
fixed head.

For competition purposes the T57S
chassis was fitted with a streamlined, all-

1 *The T57 Bugatti was produced in a number
of forms but this body, called the Atalante, was
particularly striking and must have seemed
very modern in the mid-1930s* (National
Motor Museum) 2 *The one-off SS100 Coupé,
shown at the 1938 Earls Court Show, was
Lyons' version of a developing theme among
performance car designers* (J C) 3 *Jumping
15 years ahead, one can surely detect the same
theme in the XK120 Fixed-Head Coupé, further refined* (J C) 4 *A one-off built in 1946 or
1947 shows the XK120 Roadster taking shape
in Lyons' thinking*

4

enveloping body termed the 'tank'. Notable amongst the car's successes was its triumph in the 1937 Le Mans race, when the car established a new record distance. It does not take very much imagination to notice the similarity of the 'tank' and the C-Type designed for Le Mans, particularly the ill-fated long-nose, long-tail version.

Again, and perhaps most interestingly, the Bugatti influence (or was it coincidence?) can be seen when you compare the type 101 with several Jaguar models. This T101 was to all intents and purposes a re-bodied, postwar version of the T57 and was announced in 1951, some four years after Ettore Bugatti's death. The obvious Jaguar comparison is with the 2.4 saloon, later to be augmented by the 3.4, and later still to be replaced by the MK2 range. The similarities are too obvious to need comment.

What is less well known is that during 1954, Lyons had designed a new bo for the replacement of the XK120, a it was only lack of time and staff th resulted in the 120's survival in revis form as the XK140. The prototy model was quite obviously another st in the evolution of the 'Lyons line' a can also be compared with interest.

The Bugatti/Jaguar relationship further compounded by the fact that original Bugatti-designed Bebe Peug is said to have been the inspiration

1

2

3

e Austin Seven, which was Lyons's
iginal basis.

Whatever the real sources of Lyons's
spiration, it all makes for fascinating
njecture. It may also stimulate discus-
on on the subject among enthusiasts,
cause there are plenty of them all over
e world treasuring examples of the
forgettable 'Lyons line'.

6

1, 2, 3 *Three fascinating views of a styling exercise in open and closed form. Produced probably in the mid-1950s, it may have been intended as an XK140 replacement, instead of the XK150. In it can be seen the small saloon, the XKs and even a hint of the XJC. It was a very stylish car, aided in appearance by the lack of sidelights, number plates, etc. Note the XK120 front bumpers*

4 *The path to the eventual XJ40 design was a tortuous one as Sir William's successors grappled with the problem of following his masterly XJ6. This was the thinking in 1973. (Jaguar Cars)* **5** *Three years later the styling mock-ups were still reflecting the views of the senior British Leyland management which felt that the XJ6 was too old-fashioned and the replacement must ape the more box-like Germanic creations. (Jaguar Cars)*

6

7

At the 1978 Birmingham Motor Sho[w]
Pininfarina exhibited this one-off styli[ng]
exercise based on the XJS. Later painted [in]
silver and then even more stunningly go[od-]
looking, the car was more Jaguar than the XJ[S,]
a true lineal successor to the E-type and mig[ht]
well have been accepted as the basis for the ne[w]
model had BL had the money to invest. Inste[ad]
this highly significant model remained a poin[ter]
to, and influence on, future models many yea[rs]
down the line. The still-born XJ41 sports c[ar]
project that nearly reached fruition but w[as]
killed in the early nineties, looked remarkab[ly]
akin to this XJS Spyder. One can see its distin[ct]
influence in the XJ220 and the Aston Mart[in]
DB7, while the X100, the late nineties XJ[S]
replacement will bear a resemblance. How s[ad]
that it could not have been launched in the ear[ly]
eighties, and what a difference it might ha[ve]
made to Jaguar's fortunes. (J C)

AFTERWORD

by

Nick Scheele

Chairman and Chief Executive, Jaguar Cars Ltd

hen I joined Jaguar in January 1992 no-one had prepared me
the culture shock I was about to undergo. Within days I was
are that Jaguar was a motor industry phenomenon quite
ferent to anything else I had experienced. No other car
mpany generates the same level of interest, enthusiasm and
some cases pure emotion, than Jaguar and this is reflected in
amount of media attention the Company receives. From
e to time this makes us feel we are living in a goldfish bowl
we wouldn't change it for the world!
The fact that there are so many Jaguarphiles throughout the

world, also has another side effect – a whole library of books
devoted to the marque. Amongst authors of these many books,
none is more authoritative than Philip Porter and *Jaguar – The
Complete Illustrated History*, is one of the first books I turned to
back in 1992 when I put myself through a crash course in
Jaguar culture. I hope the latest edition, which brings the
Jaguar story up to date, will be as interesting and as useful as I
found its predecessor.

Nick Scheele
March 1995

INDEX